The MANGO Story

Humberto Salerno & Andrea Gay Zaragoza

LONDON MADRID
NEW YORK MEXICO CITY
BARCELONA MONTERREY

Published by
LID Publishing Ltd.
6-8 Underwood Street
London N1 7JQ (United Kingdom)
Ph. +44 (0)20 7831 8883
info@lidpublishing.com
LIDPUBLISHING.COM

A member of BPR

businesspublishersroundtable.com

Printed in Great Britain by TJ International Ltd.

ISBN: 978-1-907794-11-7
Collection editor: Jeanne Bracken
Translation: Don Topley
Cover design: Laura Pérez Reyes
Typesetting: SyS Alberquilla S.L.

First edition: July 2011

"Regard your good name as the richest jewel you can possibly be possessed of – for credit is like fire; when once you have kindled it you may easily preserve it, but if you once extinguish it, you will find it an arduous task to rekindle it again. The way to gain a good reputation is to endeavour to be what you desire to appear."

Socrates

Contents

1 | A Success Story

Although cases of success in business should always be celebrated, today more than ever, in this climate of world economic crises, these kinds of stories are essential as models to emulate. They inspire and encourage those entrepreneurs and professionals who, exhausted by the inescapable pressures of such a complex situation, might see something of themselves in these stories and feel motivated to keep going. It can be a big boost to our best entrepreneurs, granting them a good dose of confidence for cultivating ideas to launch new projects.

But this book is not aimed at only those readers who need lessons in a better way to execute a project. There is no doubt that interested readers will also find something exciting in this story of the journey and analysis of a multinational we are all familiar with, that has become a benchmark brand in the textile business worldwide.

In these times of considerable uncertainty, good business practice proves its worthiness as a course to adopt, since we cannot ignore the fact that values are in a state of transition, and businesses are finding themselves obliged to adopt more ethical principles that embrace more than just company profit. It is precisely this philosophy that Enric Casi, Mango CEO, promotes when he states that "the aim of the company is to have a presence in every city in the world without losing sight of values that are essential in the work environment: humility, harmony and affection".

There is no doubt that Mango's success is the outcome of constant development. The Mango project is a long-term process, and this is revealed by its strategic decision-making process, as we shall see in the following pages. Something rather unusual is revealed in the history of this textile sector business. The present moment has not caused them to lose sight of their past, and Casi – who was eager for this book to be written – always insists that they should continue thinking the way a small shopkeeper does, that they should remain a local business.

This notion, which might seem rather innocent when we note the current size of the company, demonstrates a desire to control the growth model and maintain a clear awareness of where they came from and who they are.

Although the present moment is complex, it is also important to keep our eyes on the fact that for Mango, Spain's economic environment was not so easy in the 1980s when their journey began.

The company had to deal with a country splintered by years of the Franco dictatorship and a non-competitive economy with rocketing inflation, high unemployment and an exploding budget deficit, among the other problems. But this motivated the entrepreneurial spirit of the founders, Isak and Nahman Andic, impelling them to realize that they needed to gather their forces exactly at that time when it was essential for them to go against the current and seekopportunities in a market weak on exports and lacking in global awareness. Although no exact parallel exists between these two crisis situations, the fact is that economies are cyclical, and that during tough times, the ability to lead a project is most definitely tested. In those early years of Spain's dawning democracy, Spanish fashion did not dominate the international catwalks. This situation has fortunately changed over the years, and Mango has played an undeniably important role in that change.

In recent years with the aim of tackling future challenges facing the organization while pursuing its growth objectives, Mango launched an ambitious plan. Part of it has been realized through brand strengthening by using actresses with household names such as Penélope Cruz and Scarlett Johansson. This design and advertising coup led to a prestigious design prize. The structure of the company was also reorganized by creating a Board of Directors and a Management Committee, the members of which are partners in the company. A huge logistics centre in Parets del Vallés is has also been built.

With time, the Andic brothers managed to surround themselves with a great team of professionals able to consolidate a business dream with long-term aspirations and goals, not to mention internationally admired success, a subject for analysis in the business schools.

All of these efforts also garnered a great number of prizes, both for fashion and in the institutional and management field. Worth noting, among the most recent ones is an acknowledgement of Isak Andic's position as The Key to Barcelona 2008 and the Marketing Leaders Prize (professionals from 2007), awarded by the Marketing Professionals Association. Mango was also honoured by the Spanish Association for Entrepreneurial Development (AEDME) in 2008 in the Business Sponsorship and Patronage section. In 2007, the Barcelona Chamber of Commerce awarded the company the BCN Best Shop in the World Prize. And in 2009, the El Botón - Mango Fashion Awards initiative received the 'Barcelona is Fashion' prize awarded by the Barcelona Chamber of Commerce for the best company of its size, international growth and for its business strategy.

The success of the project can be measured by means of a multitude of parameters, and no doubt one of them is size. At the present moment, Mango is the number two textiles business group in Spain, just behind the giant, Inditex, with 8,600 employees on the payroll and 1,700 points of sale in a hundred-odd countries. And while those facts may be important, no less significant is Mango's outstanding capacity to set fashion trends and maintain steady growth with its extraordinary international presence.

What secrets might this pattern reveal? How did Mango manage to become a multinational in such a competitive sector as fashion?

To answer these questions we must penetrate to the heart of the company and get to know some of its managers. We must seek a better understanding of their philosophy, find out if there is something unusual about their management style, their fundamental values and how they see fashion. The scope of Mango's successful management model goes far beyond the mere notion of fashion itself, and extends to important management policies in the economic, social, labour and environmental fields. Its history shows that, apart from the company's completely natural interest in keeping abreast of the latest fashion trends, it has made significant efforts to upgrade its organizational administration procedures to the point of creating its own personality. This has meant that on many occasions Mango has outstripped the competition and the rest of the sector in areas such as new technologies or logistics. This business style has been an essential element in achieving the success reflected by positive growth in company profits year after year.

A good example of this unusual vision could be due to its managers' long-term commitment to corporate social responsibility (CSR) as an overall value, one that is essential to the company, as is their philosophy regarding work.

A swift glance at the market might lead us to conclude that consumers basically make purchases on grounds such as practicality, design and current trends. But nowadays the urge to buy is increasingly based on intangible values associated with the attitude of the company to its immediate surroundings and the environment in general.

CSR also accords with an ideal collaborative model on the part of its suppliers and employees, who see the company's success as an example to follow and are therefore proud to belong to it. In the case of Mango, it is CSR that established the collaboration relationship with its suppliers, setting down very clear standards to be adhered to, together with the responsibilities the company accepts for them. In other words, this management policy increases overall brand perception value and magnifies the yield thereby achieved.

This type of structure is of vital importance for an organization that works with 194 garment and accessories suppliers (39.7 per cent of its production comes from China), none of which operate on an exclusive basis. Subcontracting is therefore one of the most important aspects of management and at the same time, one of the most complicated to handle.

However, we must also highlight the importance of the individuals and their teamwork in an organisation that has succeeded in keeping the entrepreneurial spirit alive from day one, because their passion, feelings and excitement are still visible. Andic himself acknowledges that one of his secrets has been to allow himself to be advised by an excellent team of professionals whose aim is to be the best in their field, who strive to turn each day into a new opportunity and to completely reinvent the company every five years.

For starters, Board members eat together every day, and during that time they have the chance to air their concerns and talk about the progress they are making. According to Andic, it is this proximity between people that makes it possible for them to share information, so that nobody starts to believe that they alone are the saviour of the company.

The management team, all of whom boast an extensive professional experience with the company, is fully aware of the fact that their employees' admiration is the attracting feature in the consumer's subconscious and that it decisively affects the end product. Behind the design, the purchaser sees evidence of Mango's social commitment and quality. This exciting and enterprising mentality, and the dynamic organization of teamwork appear to add value to the end product and.In addition to this, Mango can claim to be one of the brands that has earned worldwide recognition in the fashion world among women. And it has achieved this because it has set trends, thanks to its collections.

From the beginning, it has counted on the 'personality' of its garments, attributing special significance to design and originality. Unlike its competitors, Mango continues to offer its customers the concept of exclusivity by means of carefully controlling the number of garments produced, by displaying the garments to their best advantage and by giving customers good advice. Along with the Swedish company

H&M, it offers an original product at an affordable price, although, as Enric Casi points out, "women with the Mango profile have more ambitious values."

Standing out while also adapting to shifting and fleeting trends calls for time, tenacity, flexibility, talent, and an organization that is capable of focusing its efforts on creativity. Mango has always worked this way, counting on the essential freshness of its garments.

Mango initially decided to adopt a kind of denim style, but since 1996 its collections have taken a more sophisticated and attractive direction, offering more style, while at the same time expanding its product range. In other words, the move has been towards the concept of the exclusive store and away from the image of the huge chain. Curious to note, Mango originally took chances on designs for men, women and children, but then focused on women's clothing that reflect more independent ideas and where there is greater interest in changes in trends. But now, male fashion is making a comeback to Mango.

If we accept the fact that the purpose of a trend is to influence or adapt to peoples' lifestyles, we can also confirm the fact that Mango constantly seeks to reinvent itself, adapting to multiculturalism and the actual competitive pressure found in the fashion world. And as an outcome of these permanent revolutions, in 2011, Mango will implement a very significant change in the management model which, according to forecasts, will significantly boost sales, even in the current crisis context.

To give its creations international exposure, Mango has employed a wide range of outstanding celebrities such as Scarlett Johansson, Claudia Schiffer, Naomi Campbell and Penélope Cruz, among many others. They represent the company's brand image, in keeping with feminine taste or fashion as it exists at any given moment. The company felt this was the best way to approach its female public.

In 2007, when the current crisis was just beginning to be noticed, the Catalan company decided to readapt it pricing policy with an affordably priced collection, its *Think up* line [Special prices for creative living]. However, this had little effect, reinforcing the image of the Mango purchaser as a woman for whom price is a relative value in comparison with more decisive factors such as quality and product sophistication.

Pressing forward in the search for diversification as a way of creating new opportunities, the company recently began to experiment with a collection just for men. The sales results so far are providing grounds for great growth expectations.

Our general understanding of the company now leads us to focus on its goals to become global. Mango has grasped the opportunity to grow and expand, with its presence now in over 100 countries thanks to the franchise formula (60 per cent of the brand's shops are covered by this ownership scheme at the moment) and it has activated sophisticated high volume production, warehousing and distribution systems by using the indispensable support of new technology. In actual fact, it can be said that the use of technology is one of the key points in Mango's growth strategy. The company's persistent commitment to remain in the vanguard is demonstrated by the presence of over 200 Information & Communication Technology (ICT) specialists as an element of its organizational structure. These specialists implement procedure improvements to cut delivery times and slash costs. Very little of this work is outsourced, because as with product design, it forms part of the company's exclusive and unique identity.

The distribution goal is to have 3,000 points of sale open in all five continents within the coming decade. Mango has no territorial representatives – it operates throughout the world from its head office in Palau-Solità i Plegamans (a small community near Barcelona), and it is from here that it meets its design, communication, administration and distribution needs for all the shops. When the company began to grow, it opened local offices in France and Germany, but when problems occurred and the country office was contacted, this in turn called central headquarters.

Thanks to this system they have been able to reduce structural costs and streamline day-to-day procedures. At the present time foreign sales make up 78 per cent of the total turnover, but the final goal is for them to exceed 90 per cent of sales. It is also expected that between 2010 and 2013 turnover will grow by 15 per cent annually. The last financial report (2009) showed a turnover of 1,480 million Euros for the textile business, representing a growth of 2.8 per cent compared with the previous year.

As regards production, Mango has never manufactured its garments in Spain. Presently 39.7 per cent of its production comes from China, and most of the rest from Turkey, Vietnam and North Africa.

Another of the company's strategic plans is to continue to grow its sales via the internet. This channel has huge potential for growth in the coming years, both via external platforms such as the sales website privalia.com and by means of its own corporate channel Mangoshop. com. Expert analysis of the company suggests that business growth via the internet will mainly be based on the contribution from external channels.

After 26 years, the company's entire team is excited to have fresh goals and reach for new heights. As Enric Casi, Mango CEO, says, "you have to work on the long term, because our intention is that the company will still be around many years from now." An example of this philosophy and future-focused mentality is Mango's spectacular city project, which covers an area equal to 120 football fields.Still in the development stage, apart from an industrial zone, it will include some 100,000 square metres for tertiary purposes, of which 10,000 will be for commercial objectives, with the inclusion of a discount shop of the company's products and those of other commercial brands.

However the future turns out, it will continue to be determined by the three factors that have been vital to Mango's success: the concept, the team and the possession of their own technology.

2

The Isak Andic–Enric Casi Double Act

The story of Mango is the story of entrepreneurs such as its founder, Isak Andic, or his brother Nahman, as well as the hundred of franchisees who with their faith in their company and business model, have placed their trust in the brand and made it what it is today.

Andic, born in Istanbul in 1953 to a large family with Sephardic roots, could not begin to guess about the successes which awaited him once he moved to Barcelona as a teenager. Yet it was not long after his arrival in this City of the Counts that he took his first steps in what was to be a long career by selling shirts imported from India and other Asian countries to his friends to make some extra cash while he was a student. And it was in this casual way that his relationship with the textile business was born in the 1970s, years prior to the opening of the first Mango store in Barcelona's Paseo de Gracia in 1984.

Despite his professional success and the growth of his business, Andic has always stayed aloof from communications media, and has only allowed himself to be interviewed on very few occasions. But away from the pressure of media and uncomfortable photo shoots, it turns out he is easily spotted at business events and institutional functions. Both his control of his public exposure and his business discretion are features he shares with Amancio Ortega, founder and president of the Inditex group.

Comparisons are often made between the two companies and their business models, but one thing is certain – parallels notwithstanding, their views of business are very different.

The facts tell us that Inditex is ahead of Mango on macro matters such as turnover (seven times greater), the number of shops, brand management and the size of the payroll, among other matters. The comparison can only be relative, since leaving aside gross numbers, both companies operate according to different strategies. Unlike Inditex, the company with head offices in Catalonia has concentrated on its female public, and has always banked on the creation of its own collections or expansion via franchising.

At the start of his professional career, Isak Andic was familiar with the ins and outs of the fashion industry from the wholesale side. From the premises located on Trafalgar Street in Barcelona, the current president and chief Mango shareholder used to sell the most traditional styles of various brands of denim clothes to others that he had designed and made for him by brands like Burbuja, Scooter or Mango itself. Despite how much he learned over these years, and his knowledge of the sector, it was a bittersweet experience during which the instability of the business world was consistently too risky. The gains made during three years of fruitful business could vanish in the following two. And the situation at the time presented other problems. The wholesale business kept him at a distance from the end customer, which meant that it was impossible to control market volatility and get to know the tastes and aims of his target public firsthand. Having learned his lesson, the time had come for him to seek another course and take on fresh talent to professionalize management and overcome some of those hurdles. At that time, 1983, Enric Casi was an outside consultant for the company. Born in Barcelona in 1956, he had studied Business Sciences, and at the age of 23 began to work as a consultant for Mango, among other companies. From that time on, their professional relationship grew steadily closer, until in 1989 he was appointed general manager, the position he still holds. Since 2007 when the Board of Directors was formed, Casi has also been the Group's managing director. Since 2006 he has also been a board member of the Textile Industry Research Association (AITEX) and is a regular speaker and teacher on a number of programmes at various business schools, as well as a lecturer at different centres. In 2006 he was awarded the Best External Manager Prize by the weekly financial publication *Actualidad Económica* and in the following year he was honoured as Manager of the Year 2006, a title awarded by the Spanish Association of Managers.

His youth was no handicap to his decision-making skills when the time came for Enric Casi to tackle the strategic changes that the company had yet to undergo. One of the first responsibilities he and the Mango team had to take on at the crucial moment of transformation from wholesaler to direct retailer was to decide who their target public was and how they should focus on them.

At that time there was little in the way of information media which meant it was difficult to obtain and process reliable market information. At that time the team held quarterly meetings to analyze the information they could obtain and plan the direction they would pursue for the following three months.

In 1984 the company was ready to take an important step forward in its development – the opening of its first shop in the central Paseo de Gracia shopping area. This was the beginning of what we would now call the Mango model.

Since by that time they had decided to focus exclusively on women's fashion, they were prepared to fine-tune their market to a specific type of woman, and from then on their customer would be modern, young, self-confident, even daring – someone interested in looking her best who was always on the lookout for the latest fashion statement. The inspiration for the brand name had appeared years before on a trip Isak Andic took to the Philippines in the 1970s. In his opinion the mango fruit has a certain exotic quality, it is sensual, has the feeling of freshness and is associated with pleasant emotions ... all ideas they would seek to transmit to the women the company intended to dress.

Once they decided to abandon men's and children's fashion, a last minute decision, they staked everything on women as the focus of their business. This has defined the Mango story almost up until this very moment, when they are now seeking to reposition themselves by extending their base into the design and sale of men's fashion.

After these first strategic changes, their next step was clear, and by 1985 Mango already had five points of sale in Barcelona. This expansion of the company to the rest of the country began in Valencia. What had at first been just a small group of colleagues grew, and in 1988 the company had thirteen points of sale. Once the brand had been consolidated in the domestic market, they began their international expansion with the opening of two stores in Portugal. It was in that very year that Mango launched store number 100 in Spain.

Now that its pattern for success was consolidated, the company underwent some changes in its basic structure in 1996 that was designed to help it sustain growth through the coming years. International expansion became an important aspect of Mango, and an ambitious plan was outlined whereby they would open at least 100 stores per year. Over time, the company launched between 150 and 200 shops per year until they reached almost 1,400 in 2009. The current rate of store opening is an average of eight points of sale per week.

In 1996, when the Mango payroll was just 100 strong, it demonstrated a clear intention to keep on growing at an almost exponential rate. However, it was clear that in order to keep this up a great deal of reorganization would be needed and the structure which would steer that growth would have to be defined very clearly. It was at that time that Mango established its unique style, such as the fact that development would have to rest on a network of its own shops as well as franchised businesses. Isak Andic defined that moment very precisely in one of his few interviews, when he stated that "what matters is a firm grip on the concept, but the formulae must be allowed to develop."

With this in mind we can now see that the history of the company is divided into two parts. The first part covers the first eleven years, the period when Mango was learning the business and getting to know the sector well enough to consolidate new work procedures allowing for growth in the future. One example of this is the just-in-time philosophy in its distribution and production areas, which allowed the company to be more effective and maintain a consistent standard of quality while taking fewer risks.

Part two runs from 1996 to the present time. This is a period during which the values of the individuals involved have been reinforced with the aim of increasing investment in a new concept of integrated logistics and developing the franchise side of the business. Efficiency, expansion and technology are some of the characteristic features of Mango's business maturity over these years.

During this time, the company Andik founded has opened larger stores and has been growing abroad. This is how Enric Casi sums up the new philosophy of the company he manages: "In the context in which we find ourselves, the success of our company is based on three factors: the concept of the product, the people and technology. The latter two points are fundamental, because they are something the others can't copy from you." The result of Mango's two phases of growth is an industrial model which reaches further than traditional patterns. It has pursued a business culture of its own based on the knowledge society. This is how the company has managed to create a competitive production system rooted in innovation and technology as added values.

Andic as the businessmen's leader

In 2010 Andic was elected president of the Family Business Institute in Spain, an organization which includes all the greatest companies in this country and which, since its foundation in 1992, has influenced the economic policy of a succession of governments (at national as well as regional and local levels). There is no doubt that this appointment not only increases the visibility and public awareness of Mr. Andic, a genuine self-made man, but also his responsibility to the business community.

3

Mango in the Context of Fashion

A good starting point for understanding what constitutes a company and what position it occupies in the sector where it operates is to analyze all the aspects of its situation with a view to achieving a true and accurate picture of what really lies behind the logo.

We should begin by defining what Mango means in the fashion industry. Fashion businesses can be classified according to various parameters. We might, for example, examine the relationship between the nature of the organization and the style of the product it markets, because although there are no obvious connections between one and the other in the eyes of the layman, fashion creation and design processes depend, to a considerable extent, on the kind of business that develops them.

This leads us to identify the businesses that give precedence to emotional response, companies at the top where creativity and artistic freedom are priorities. The creative directors of these brands have a public relevance greater than the managers, executives and in some cases the owners themselves. This category includes fashion houses such as Gucci or Yves Saint Laurent.

Then there are rational or mass production companies. These kinds of organizations see their management models as more important than the design of their collections, and creativity and design are subordinated to the company's commercial objectives. Here we find businesses such as Inditex and H&M.

Another criterion we might use to classify fashion companies might be the part the designer plays in the organization. This classification covers companies run by designer-entrepreneurs (Armani, for example), businesses in which the designers are creative directors for very well-known brands (such as Karl Lagerfeld for Chanel) and organizations which include designers who work anonymously for a brand and are subject to the supervision of those managing the company's image.

With these criteria in mind, we would position Mango in the category of rationally organized companies with anonymous designers. This classification places the targeted public as the focus of creativity, since design should be adapted to their tastes with efforts made to establish trends that are not excessively distant from the end customer's desires. This is in contrast to the emotionally-organized companies where it is the designers who dictate trends independently, sometimes in a very avant-garde and daring way, that customers may or may not follow.

In this light, Mango has perfectly defined its target public – the young modern, urban woman we mentioned before – with whom it can build a relationship based on its own designs that follow the latest trends.

1. Creating and identifying trends

What then, are the keys to this relationship? How are the connections between the company and its public built? For Mango to detect what creates demand, structures are initiated to monitor the main sources of inspiration in design, that take on the form of players involved in the world of the fashion creation world.

Initially we look at the trend laboratories, businesses which specialize in identifying trends by observing society. They employ specialist staff who look out for trends that spontaneously appear on any street in the world. They also monitor the latest medical, scientific and technological developments that might also define and create a trend. The customers of these laboratories are big fashion houses working in *haute couture* and middle range or cosmetics companies, all seeking valuable information for creating successful designs and appropriately planning production procedures. If they are aware of the trends, they can minimize risk. But the designers complain that the advice that comes from these laboratories often leads to a loss of creativity in their work. Trend Union, Nelly Rodi, Peclers Paris and WGSN are some of the main agents at the international level.

Just as important are the *haute couture* houses that set trends with their designs and their emotional appeal. Fashion shows are social and media events that reveal what will be worn in the coming season, creating currents of influence that define what will really succeed in the immediate future.

At the professional level, a close watch is also kept on innovations from what are known as primary-level companies – businesses that produce materials such as fibre laboratories or manufacturers of yarns and fabrics, who test the market with their developments with a margin of some 24 months lead time before they can be used to manufacture the end products. Cotton Incorporated is an example of this type of company.

Sector-based fairs are also sources of inspiration that are important for companies like Mango. They are a meeting place for fabric manufacturers, designers, trendspotting professionals known as 'coolhunters' and so on. Worthy of note because of the range of objectives and target publics is Première Vision, held twice-yearly in Paris and New York, a benchmark fair for the most important producers in the world. Here fabrics, materials, couture and prints that will set the trends for the following year can be spotted. Producers show and sell their work here with an eye on the season's catwalks. Other outstanding fairs are Bread&Butter and Pitti Filati. The former, which started in Berlin and was held on several occasions in Barcelona, focuses on trends in emerging brands and commercial brands. The latter fair, held in Florence, is seen as a laboratory and observatory for the most innovative trends throughout the world in the area of yarns for knitwear.

Companies that make their products available to the consumer also have a direct influence on trends. This is a very heterogeneous group ranging from companies that finish off the materials from primary level businesses to organizations that buy the finished products directly, and could include multibrand businesses, large store fashion departments, clothing chains, sales outlets, etc.

The fact that the media hold two levels of influence should also be borne in mind. On the one hand there are sector-based publications that boost relationships between the various players and serve fashion businesses by detecting trends at any level *(Women's World Daily* and *MModa* are two good examples); and on the other are the general media which function as external agents. In other words, publications can become factors that have a decisive effect on a collection or a product, although the same can also be said of other kinds of cultural influences, such as films, music or shows. The upshot is that a whole season may be completely changed by the unexpected success of a film, as happened with *Out of Africa* (the film starring Robert Redford and Meryl Streep), which changed the tones and colours that had been forecast for that summer into safari shades, as Santa Bertomeu, a lecturer at the European Institute of Design pointed out.

In any case, fashion as a phenomenon is not separate from society; it is a part of our everyday life, and this means that any chance event might alter its course. For example, in September 2001 during the Première Vision fair, the trend was towards textiles, prints and designs with Arab motifs. The attack on the Twin Towers in New York that same year eliminated any reference to these types of designs with a single stroke, driven by the general rejection of anything to do with the Arab world at that time.

2. Interpreting trends

Identifying and describing trends is just the first step in the creation of a product. Interpretation, the next step, is dominated by in-house factors at work in each company, the style code, and external factors, which involve positioning or the viewpoint of third parties. In all cases, the ideal is to seek a balance between both aspects, and in this respect Mango is no exception. On the one hand, its designs must comply with the actual factors that make up the essential Mango, based on satisfying an avant-garde public who want to stand out but at a reasonable price; and on the other, they must reflect external and seasonal elements based on the trends for each season.

The external factors are very important to Mango. They are identified from the trend laboratories' style notebooks, from the quest for shops or niche markets in the world's most fashion-conscious cities, such as New York, London, Paris or Stockholm, from sector fairs and from specialist blogs, etc. At the same time, the company must strive to position itself as an external factor in the creation of trends by investing in the organization of fashion shows, which also have an effect on the re-evaluation of its designs.

All the external factors are monitored by the design coordination department which works with the trends and establishes new guidelines. It is this department that provides the teams with all the relevant information.

We can distinguish four different levels of retail trades in the fashion sector according to their power to set trends:

- *Haute couture*: powerful trendsetters. *Haute couture* is seen as the laboratory of fashion, where designers can experiment with almost total freedom with materials, lines and styles;

- Read-to-wear fashion: this is seen as the democratization of fashion and made its appearance after World War II, when the consumer society began to demand fashion and design at reasonable prices. At this time big firms began to present more profitable mass-produced collections;

- Continuous production companies: mass-target fashion houses such as Zara or Mango, which also offer trends, thanks to rapid design and promotion cycles that they implement for them;

- Off-the-peg or short-circuit clothes businesses: garments that are usually sold in multibrand shops.

**Figure 3.1 Levels of trend creation according to point
of sale type.**

Source: Santa Bertomeu / Own research.

The Ailanto case: the other side of the coin

To understand the influence that trends can have on fashion brands, it is interesting to take a look at a different business model such as Ailanto, a company with good connections but which operates on more emotional rather than rational strategies.

Ailanto is a fashion company located in Barcelona which was set up in 1992 by Iñaki and Aitor Muñoz. Unlike the majority of companies in the sector, the Muñoz brothers base their designs not on trends but on their own style code. The Ailanto look is distinguished by exclusive prints, a taste for classical designs and the constant use of colour. With this in mind we should position the company as much in the middle as at the top of the pyramid shown in figure 3.1.

> This greater creative freedom implies a certain level of concessions made to economic objectives. In their case, sales do not influence designs, and this allows them to follow their own inclinations in the world of fashion.

3. The design team at Mango

As CEO Enric Casi puts it, creativity is Mango's *raison d'être*. Responsibility for creativity is in the hands of the designers, which means that both parties see this operation as one of the fundamental pillars of the company. Design is not an exclusive element of garment production, since it goes further than this and influences other processes, such as the points of sale themselves, where Mango takes responsibility for every individual item, from the window displays to the bags in which the customers carry away their purchases, and including the catalogue and interior design of the shops and the windows.

The design team is organized into different areas, depending on the kind of fabric they are working with. This means that it is broken up into the plain, knitted, round knit, denim and power T-shirt sections. In the case of the plain, knitted and round knit teams they are subdivided into casual and suit categories.

Unlike other brands, Mango groups its garments into four collections. Each projects a unique brand image that is unified and consistent, so that the resulting garments transmit the company style. The collections are standardized for their entire customer base with the exception of some adaptations for groups of countries with different traditions, such as Arab or Asian regions. Variations also occur within the general collection to cope with the climatic features of certain regions.

The collections are made up of two types of products: historical or perpetual (basic or semi-basic lines with slight modifications), and renewed (associated with trends). The difference whena renewed design moves on to become historical is revealed by the sales volume figures achieved.

Apart from the designs which make up the general collection, Mango launches special garments for collections outside the established seasons:

- New arrivals: small collections of five or six garments that are launched shortly before the arrival of the general collection at the shop;

- Reprise: garments that have to reach the stores quickly since they are expressions of trends and add freshness to the collections.

The new design creation procedure at Mango is divided into nine steps:

1. Design: research, fabrics, colours and sketches;

2. Reception of samples and selection: first prototypes;

3. Quotation: designs are adjusted to suit budgets according to materials and negotiations with suppliers;

4. Purchasing (quantities and colours of each model);

5. Presentation at the fashion show (if there is one);

6. Pre-production;

7. Production;

8. Distribution;

9. Display at the shop.

Abiding by predetermined process times, the team works with the collection on a six months lead time basis.

Once the garment has been designed and purchased, the follow-up team perfects the design and scales it up and down to all sizes. When the collections have already been launched, the product managers distribute the garments (or accessories) to the various regions according to the information gleaned from market research and monitoring studies that reflect the ways in which the products function for each one.

The effect of the crisis on fashion from the experts' point of view.

Leonard Lauder, ex-president of cosmetics company Estée Lauder, recounts that "sales [of the products of the brand] have undergone significant growth at times of crisis, such as during the Great Depression of 1929 to 1933, the post-war period or the 9/11 attacks in 2001." This is due to the fact that at times of crisis, when expenses seen as unnecessary tend to be eliminated, a kind of monotony is experienced by the public who areaffected by the dullness of the environment, and tend to seek gratification from small purchases such as a lipstick (and in actual fact, the lipstick index is used as an indicator of historical times of crisis).

Santa Bertomeu comments that "at the emotional and consumer level, crisis has a positive effect, and generates conscious consumption." Bartomeu also states that, "although they may not be affected in a direct way, the pressure from around them to be more careful with their spending makes people feel as though they have been contaminated by the crisis phenomenon, and they rationalize this. The upshot is that they cut down on impulse buying (in the case of what is known as Zara addicts) and purchase garments of better quality."

However, in the context of a crisis, Bartomeu supports the thesis that design shows signs of a negative effect. As far as this particular expert, with more than 30 years in the profession, is concerned, "if we take into account the low level of creativity in our country, company managers' fear of taking risks has hindered their development even more. This sets up a vicious circle which affects supply and becomes reality when a consumer goes into a shop and sees the same designs season after season."

As far as Aitor Muñoz of Ailanto is concerned, he believes that because of the crisis "aesthetic suggestions are less radical" and that brands have been forced to lower their prices to remain competitive, which has further repercussions on the costs of the fabrics or the number of garments produced.

4

The Development of a Universal Brand

The success of Mango as a company is concealed behind a blend of effective logistics and production policies, accurate strategies in expansion projects and a researched brand image that extends from the design of the collection to the smallest detail of the interior decoration of the stores. Even so, as Enric Casi himself concedes, there are no perfect recipes for all situations. The growth and positioning of his brand are based on a very personal business model and product where every department in the company is involved.

Even so, a degree of loyalty to the fundamental values of the brand has been retained, and these values have remained in position since the definition of the Mango brand after Andic's trip to the Philippines. From the 1980s until the present moment their brand image has been associated with energy, freshness and modernity: since its inception Mango has been a company that always insists on the most up-to-date styles and materials.

With these features as the signature of its identity, the company has identified with an urban, independent female public aged 25 to 45 with medium-to-high range purchasing power. In recent years the association of its brand's values with this segment of the public has given rise to what is known as the Mango woman. But this was not always the case.

After the early years, when design was targeted at the adolescent consumer, the company focused on a more mature public and a more loyal consumer. Throughout its company history, Mango has never ceased to polish and reinforce the reliability of its personality, and has extended its collection to dress women at any time and on any occasion in their lives (work, parties, holidays, etc.). In all cases, Mango bases itself as much on the latest trends as on basic garments for a woman's core wardrobe.

At the point of sale, the company has resisted the temptation of abandoning the spirit of the small and welcoming shop for women (what we call the boutique feel) that it has depended on since the start. The way in which the shops have the personality of a small and exclusive business, even though they represent a huge organization, is a key point in Mango's strategy and the way it perceives business. Along with the creation of its own collections comes this dedication to personalized service that, in the opinion of Enric Casi, is what distinguishes Mango from the competition. Of course, controlling prices in order to reach the greatest possible number of consumers is also central to the business.

In this company, innovation and design go hand in hand and are nourished by a constant flow of information arriving from a variety of sources. One of the most important sources is their chain of stores. Direct, daily contact with customers provides valuable information that is heeded when the time comes to make decisions regarding both design and the marketing and distribution channels. None of the data Mango receives is ignored, and every variable is examined to check whether it can subsequently be applied for the benefit of a product. To process the information, the organization provides a platform where employees from various sections can add information and later recover it in line with established in-house codes.

This exchange of information benefits the company and also the suppliers, since it allows them to access information concerning the company or their products. For example, footwear suppliers can see from the platform how shoe sales are going, which means they can improve their productivity and anticipate orders to meet the needs of the company, consequently saving time.

Mango's expansion and outstanding position in the fashion industry are also due to its ability to adapt to each market, without abandoning its own identity. The Catalan company has made the "We're global because we're local" slogan its own, and the outcome has been that some 20 per cent of its collections are adapted to the tastes, customs and culture of the public for whom they are intended. For example, skirts are lengthened for collections planned for Moslem countries. Leather is the material that holds sway in designs intended for Nordic consumers, while the southeast Asian market is supplied with a greater quantity of light fabrics, such as silks.

This mentality, which is very deeply embedded in the company ethos, has turned Mango into a universal brand that crosses frontiers, but that is snugly adapted to the specific requirements of each region, a factor that allows for constant expansion under practically all conditions. An example would be the late 2009 opening of its first shop in Iraq with an area of 400 square metres, in the Kurdish province of Erbil. With the addition of this point of sale, Mango now has a presence in all the countries of the Middle East, where its first shop open in March 1997 in Kuwait.

Mango's firm decision to target emerging markets in general and the Arab world in particular takes the form of 37 shops in Saudi Arabia, 15 in the United Arab Emirates and seven in Kuwait. This market now makes up 9 per cent of the company's global turnover and the first store for Yemen has also been planned.

As you may imagine, the geographical location of the various points of sale is not arbitrary. We have already mentioned the fact that shops are a source of information for the company, so their location is always strategic. The first opening in the bustling Paseo de Gracia in Barcelona had already revealed the importance Mango was to associate with the locations of its points of sale.

Collaboration between the departments is fundamental, as mentioned earlier, for the appropriate management of information gleaned from the shops. Customer complaints, comments and suggestions always pass through the customer service department which is able to offer its services in five official languages (Spanish, Catalan, English, French and German).

In 2009, a total of 79,818 requests were handled (60,823 in 2007), and the main communications channels used were email and the company website (58 per cent), telephone calls (38 per cent), conversations in chatrooms (3 per cent) and letters and faxes (1 per cent). Consultations came directly from customers, the shops and the staff at the head office. According to type of consultation, the first reason for making contact with the company was a request for information (80 per cent), followed by complaints (19 per cent), congratulations (0.5 per cent) and suggestions (0.5 per cent).

Mango's concern for and attention to its shops also extends to its approach to its window displays. The standard for the company is that all the display windows, whether company-owned or franchises, should present consistent overall decoration and communicate the same brand image. In the chapter on franchising we shall deal with this matter, a key point for franchisees, in greater detail.

As with any industry, the success of the company derives from the talent of its members, so in recent years Mango has made efforts to attract young people with a gift for fashion who also turn out to be excellent product consultants for a younger audience. It was to promote just this talent that in November 2006 the company created the El Botón-Mango Fashion Awards, the first Spanish prize intended to support young talent in international fashion. This initiative relies on the support of first-rate co-organizers such as the Central Saint Martins School of Art and Design in London, the French Fashion Institute in Paris, the Marangoni Institute in Milan, the Antwerp Royal Academy of Fine Arts and the Higher School of Design in Barcelona, five of the most prestigious design institutes in Europe.

The competition's jury also consists of personalities from the world of fashion and has included designers of the stature of Valentino, Óscar de la Renta and Jean Paul Gaultier as presidents, plus representatives from the schools mentioned above, directors of fashion magazines, representatives from Mango such as Isak Andic or Damián Sánchez (top executive responsible for corporate image), famous fashion critics, the winner of the previous El Botón-MFA prize and reputed photographers.

Mango makes use of the world's top professionals in design to achieve international projection for its brand. It also selects its people with great care and counts on the support of international schools and experts from the sector. Argentinean Carla Hoet, joint creator with Carlos Estrada of the company HOET and professor at the Accademia del Lusso di Milano fashion school, took part in the third awarding of this prize, and stated that "the el Botón-Mango Fashion Awards is an excellent opportunity for young designers' chances of attracting international renown. There is no doubt about the importance of the competition, one of the most prestigious internationally."

Txell Miras, fashion designer and creator of her own brand, was the only Spaniard among the ten finalists in the first year the competition was held. Apart from her statement that "it is of the greatest importance that big firms of the size of Mango should establish this kind of initiative", Miras added that "without any need to do so and making use of top class professionals, Mango has created a competition which is a benchmark among international fashion prizes."

The importance and international impact of this prize call for detailed organization requiring an entire year of work. During this period the latest competition details and news are presented to the media, who broadcast the names of the first candidates and start leaking the names of the finalists before the big day when the prizes are presented.

Participants for a period of 18 months, the winners of the first two competitions were the Belgian design partnership, Sandrina Fasoli and Michaël Marson, and Korean Lee Jean Youn. The prize represents a contract to create a collection for Mango like the one produced by the young Korean designer in 2010, and a cash award of €300,000, the highest prize yet offered in this kind of competition.

There is no doubt that by upgrading the sector modeled on Mango's success sets it apart from its competitors. Juanma Granero (from the company Juanma by El Cuco), a professional who has worked with designers of the stature of Josep Font and was involved in the third competition, states that "the artistic, non-commercial nature of the competition differentiates it from other types of competitions at the same level, and endows Mango designs with special value compared with other similar brands."

Another way in which Mango has strengthened the value of its brand is by forging links with the images of international icons (mainly models and actresses). The image of these models is closely associated with Mango and its message. Such personalities have transmitted Mango's essence throughout its history, adapting to suit the values of the time. They have agreed to add their faces to an advertising campaign not just because of their beauty, but also as an embodiment of the feminine values that echo their public goals. The most recent image icon is Scarlett Johansson, one of the most renowned international actresses of our times, who for the third time has been involveed with Mango to present the spring 2010 season.

Model Claudia Schiffer, who starred in campaigns between 1992 and 1995, Naomi Campbell, Christy Turlington and Eva Herzigova were famous faces associated with the brand, particularly in the 1990s. During that decade the very best supermodels were featured in Mango's catalogues, and thanks to that, they boosted Mango's international presence. The new century brought with it new partnerships with Maja Latinovic, Inés Sastre, Karolina Kurkova, Milla Jovovich and again, Claudia Schiffer.

More recent times have welcomed celebrities from a new generation, such as Lizzy Jagger, Alice Dellal and Dakota Johnson, plus dedicated actresses or models of the ilk of Elisabeth and Lauren Hutton. In this way the Mango concept has been associated with a broad range of famous personalities who have shaped the times, and who themselves have changed to meet the contexts and needs expressed by women.

Events also form an indispensable part of the Catalan group's promotional activities. At the beginning of 2010 and for the first time, Mango participated in the World Boutique of Hong Kong Fashion Week, autumn-winter 2010-2011, organized each season by the Hong Kong Trade Development Council (HKTDC). This is the most important fashion event in Asia, and is particularly important for the textile company since this former British colony is the gateway to mainland China, where Mango already has 70 points of sale.

In November 2006, Mango held its first fashion show, introducing the spring-summer 2007 collection. Since that time it has organized two shows per year, and although they were initially held in Barcelona, in

2009 they were moved to Madrid to achieve better media exposure. In the future, the company does not exclude the possibility of organizing fashion shows in other foreign cities to keep pace with its international expansion. These shows are a very good business move, as Aitor Muñoz from Ailanto points out: "Having begun to present its collections at fashion shows has been a step forward for the brand at the international level."

As an innovator in the sector, Mango is once more helping with the birth of talent by organizing a Master's Degree in Management for Fashion and Design in collaboration with the Catalan school, Escola Superior de Disseny Industrial (ESDi). As an added value, this specialized course offers the experience gleaned from two sources of huge importance in the fashion industry: ESDi's twenty years of instruction in fashion and design, and the nearly three decades of experience that Mango has accrued.

The target public for the Master is university graduates in fashion design or textiles and management sciences eager to expand their knowledge in the management of fashion products and businesses. It is also aimed at professionals already connected with the textile sector who would like to extend and update their education by studying new management techniques and the markets.

As Enric Casi explains, "the Master is structured in three parts: first, the design and collection management process run by ESDi; second, a program focused on marketing and advertising run by the Universitat Autònoma de Barcelona, and third, learning about economic, financial, distribution and point-of-sale management headed up by Mango."

Apart from all this, as we have already pointed out, Mango's promotional activities have also affected its growth. At the present time the company is staking a great deal on street marketing actions, bringing fashion to the street with advertising exhibitors showing their collections or with the huge, attractive bags which they have positioned in front of their shops at the end of the street. All these actions, together with other more traditional examples – in advertising as well as communication, have been fundamental for the creation of their brand image. As advertising expert Kevin Roberts, world CEO of Saatchi &

Saatchi, acknowledges: "for the big brands to survive nowadays they must create loyalty (emotion) ahead of reason (rationality), because this is the only way they can distinguish themselves from millions of bland brands with no future. Products and experiences must be created that are capable of forging deep and lasting emotional bonds (which breed loyalty) with their consumers."

In today's context, where less personal mass-production prevails, and with high product turnover, Mango has managed to strengthen those emotional bonds with its customers by means of the values that the brand imbues its products with. The blend of all of these ingredients represents their ability to create a powerful brand with a great personality that stands out from the competition. In other words, the company strategy is based on the offer of good design at a good price, while others are counting on merely offering a product at a good price, leaving design to trail behind.

As we can see, a strategy which hits the target is no chance event, and this has raised the Catalan company to position 15 in the European classification of the best distribution brands, according to *Best Retail Brands 2009.* This report, published in May 2009 by the consultancy Interbrand, surveys the main consumer brands of the world and works out an evaluation position for each brand, with different editions for North America and Europe.

In the European grading, three companies which belong to the Forum of Renowned Spanish Brands, Zara, El Corte Inglés and Mango, appear among the top 17 and these are three of the four Spanish brands which figure in the first 25 positions.

5

Influence of Celebrities and Opinion Leaders

There is no doubt that product consultants or opinion leaders are a key public for companies that specialize in marketing consumer goods, since the speed with which their opinions reach the general audience boosts profits.

The effect of celebrities has a great deal to do with the theory of influence, which sees fashion as a vertical phenomenon. According to this perception, trends begin with the wealthier classes who at first are the only ones who can afford *haute couture*. Subsequently, and little by little, the price of these garments begins to fall (via similar models or directly via copies) so that when these fashions reach the street level, the personalities who dictate fashion automatically lose interest and they cease to be a trend. This law of influence is known as the trickle-down effect.

However, at present, this theory is not sufficient to explain the circuit of influences as it reaches the consumers. For example, opinion leaders are now no longer just the famous or public personalities associated with show business, sport or music. The definition of an opinion leader has expanded to include professionals of recognized standing in their fields (doctors, lawyers or politicians, for example) or an individual with authority in a given area – someone who is listened to in a variety of forums and whose opinion is sought on the widest possible range of matters. In order to be regarded as such, these opinion leaders must possess the ability to transmit the influence of what they say to an area other than what made them famous.

To achieve this, they must be regarded as having charisma and possessing sincerity, because without these qualities they can never have any influence on others. This is not the same as a product consultant, because product consultants are much closer to peoples' everyday lives, people we trust and from whom we seek advice. A product consultant could be anyone from a chemist to the woman who owns a shop in the neighbourhood.

There is no doubt that such personalities are indispensable as far as fashion houses are concerned, since they depend on them to reassure their audience about the quality of their products. This endows them with authority in the eyes of the public, who prefer to associate a purchase with a familiar face when it comes to deciding on a brand.

1. The celebrity phenomenon: the development of a concept

Montse Escobar, an expert in communication and influence with the Grey advertising agency, explained that while the use of popular personalities in advertising was nothing new, it was at the end of the 20th century that it became a fashion: "In the 1990s it became fashionable to contract celebrities who possessed considerable visibility in the media, usually from the elites of sectors such as show business, culture or sport, and who became a regular resource for public relations agencies and departments looking to achieve swift impact in communications media. Indeed, it was often the celebrities themselves who were seeking an opportunity to appear in the media."

Successful designers like Roberto Cavalli, with 40 years of experience in the world of *haute couture*, have no doubt about the association of their brand image with celebrities when it comes to communications and market penetration. The Florentine designer says that "it is beyond doubt that when a celebrity appears on the red carpet wearing one of my garments, the brand soars like a rocket, more than you would believe."[1]

Even so, as the years have passed, the phenomenon of celebrity has lost some of its credibility. This is partly because they lend their image to a number of brands, and partly because consumers are aware of the fact that the brands pay them to talk up those brands in the media.

Coincidentally, the same thing is happening with traditional messages developed by market research departments and traditional communication media (television, press, etc.) and new media (blogs, social networks, etc.). In other words, whether it is because the public is better educated and knows more about the mechanisms at work in the marketplace, or because the brands themselves have reached their saturation points, the fact is that it is becoming increasingly difficult for brands to achieve both penetration and credibility for their messages.

At the beginning of this century a new phenomenon appeared in the United States that brands in all sectors would eventually make use of. This is the the blog which has since then become increasingly important. These are open-access communication channels on the internet, based on free websites with content generally created or published by a single individual, usually updated on a daily basis. Thanks to the explosion of this phenomenon, anybody can open and maintain a personal, group or corporate space that is visible worldwide. This clearly did not go unnoticed by fashion industry companies who began introducing the word 'blog' in their communication strategies.

Now we can say that it is obvious that the internet and new media have transformed the sector, but that transformation is merely a reflection of something deeper, which is, as Domenico Dolce and Stefano Gabbana, of Dolce & Gabbana have recognized, "... if it is the case that blog authors are now in the front line next to commercial media, it's because there is a reason. It is possible to think that it is merely an aspect of democracy, but it is more than that. What it means is that the rules of the game are really changing"

The rules of the game really *are* changing, and we now talk about the influence of the non-elite on consumers. Some people have described it as the 'trickle across' theory, which means the spread of the influence of fashion from any direction or social grouping, whether vertical or horizontal.

Figure 5.1 Horizontal & Vertical Influences on Consumers.

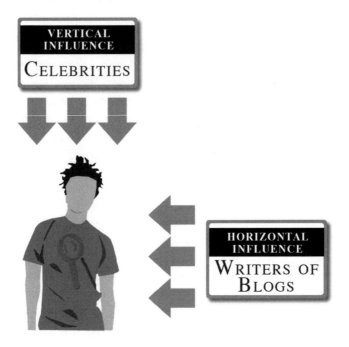

For the first time, digital communication is setting trends and it is traditional media which is dragging behind. The celebrities are losing their power and influence when they come up against the consumers, and they are yielding to new opinion leaders and product consultants. Bloggers are emerging as a new group knownas the Einstein generation (born between 1988 and now), defined by Jeroen Boshma and Inez Groen who coined the term, as "cleverer, faster and more social". According to Montse Escobar, the people who make up this group "don't allow themselves to be influenced by the famous. Their friends, companions or the people who write the blogs are the people who have the most effect on their purchasing decisions, while traditional celebrities appeal more to the older consumer."

The Blog Phenomenon:
Tavi Gevinson and Cheng Guorong

Although celebrities still carry weight when it comes to influencing consumers, these days fashion spreads in all directions. An example would be the huge influence exerted over consumers by anonymous individuals who have become opinion leaders, such as Tavi Gevinson, "the most influential girl in fashion", or the Chinese beggar Cheng Guorong, converted into an icon for Asian fashion thanks to a chance photograph.

As is usual in the lives of great celebrities, for Tavi Gevinson, author of the blog *Style Rookie* [thestylerookie.com], it is quite normal to be invited and appear in the much sought-after first row of the most important catwalks in the world, such as Milan, New York, Paris, London or Tokyo. Apart from attending a large number of runway shows, this child – only fourteen years old – takes part in lots of interviews and poses for photo sessions that the media have battled over, apart from giving her opinion to the great fashion companies of today.

On the other hand, Cheng Guorong, the Chinese beggar who became a real phenomenon thanks to the internet, has appeared in blogs, fashion magazines and newspapers as the man with the most seductive and attractive style in the world.

This young man known as the Handsome Beggar rocketed to fame by pure chance when a young girl who had just bought a camera took several photographs of him as she was leaving a shop which she then posted on one of the most popular internet forums in China.

Not only was he a resounding success in China, but his image crossed borders to the extent that he appeared on the cover of fashion magazines and was turned into an icon of Asian beauty.

Both cases are significant examples of how traditional vertical communication has become ineffective; it is amazing to think that these celebrities have more followers than many stars from the worlds of cinema or music, for example.

2. Choosing the celebrity

You would not be surprised to hear that choosing the face which will represent the values of a brand is no easy task and that a large number of factors influence that decision.

According to Alberto Alonso, a market research professional with the Danone Group, when it comes to staking everything on the image of a star, "there are three important factors. First, the person you choose must be very well known, second, they must have impact, either at the visual level (recognition) or just because of their name, depending on the aim of the campaign. And third, apart from the relevance of their field, it's important to bear in mind the values they embody and which they will bring to the brand." Starting from the assumption that the end consumer is seeking to identify with the personal characteristics of the celebrity, to incorporate their personality, it is of utmost importance that a certain affinity or connection be created between the values of the brand and those projected by the chosen individual.

Alonso also states that "the celebrity must reflect the values of the brand, must add credibility to the product with which they are associated." In other words, there must be a positive correlation between the product and the person who represents it. To guarantee results and minimize risk, many companies choose to do market research with consumers before launching their advertising campaigns.

Alonso cautions that "association with celebrities may give rise to a risk for the brand, since once the association is in place, the company will then have to manage the image of the celebrity with great care." An example of this would be golfer Tiger Woods, who lost huge advertising contracts with companies like Accenture and Gillette when his personal image collapsed in the wake of press publication of the sex scandals in which he was involved. It is important not to ignore any of these factors as far as the brands are concerned, because making the wrong choice will be a disaster in both the short and long term.

Of equal importance with the choice of face for a campaign is the way it is handled to ensure that it is consistent and continuous over time. The use of celebrities is an easy way to access mass media and hence end consumers, but that influence means there is more to be done. A brand may appear in the magazines thanks to the presence of some famous individual at the runway shows, and this may create a spike in sales, but this is a one-off phenomenon that has no effect on brand's penetration into the market in the long term.

Globalization and its homogenizing effect have worked in favour of international companies in their choice of celebrities, since as a general rule, their strategies are global. Given the cost of hiring these people, we can be certain that this type of campaign is only within the reach of big companies.

These collaboration initiatives between a famous individual and a commercial brand are not only good for the company, but for the personality, too, since the brand strategy will also boost and groom their image, reinforcing it in the public eye.

3. Collaborative arrangements between celebrities and fashion companies

A variety of different arrangements exist between fashion firms and celebrities. In the case of Mango, these arrangements have operated in a variety of fields, from design, with the creation of special collections, to advertising, with the use of the celebrity's image in the campaigns.

a) Collaboration with celebrities to develop specific collections

This can be seen as a brand creation strategy in which the celebrities act as the actual brands. These collaborations are usually organized with significant individuals from the worlds of music, film, sport or fashion.

The company H&M was a pioneer in the democratization of *haute couture* designs when it offered them to the general public via its collaborations with great designers and creative managers such as Karl Lagerfeld, Stella McCartney, Roberto Cavalli, Jimmy Choo and Sonia Rykiel, among others. The experience was satisfactory to both parties involved, because the designers were delighted to see queues of customers in front of the shops before they opened, knowing that they would run out of stock in a matter of minutes. The Swedish company has also collaborated with names from show business, such as Madonna or Kylie Minogue.

For some years now, Mango has worked with celebrities like Milla Jovovich, Elizabeth Hurley or Penélope and Mónica Cruz to create special collections. The company discovered this formula for success when it organized a cautious collaborative arrangement with Milla Jovovich, who was already the brand's representative image. Subsequently it repeated the experiment with the Cruz sisters and Elizabeth Hurley.

It has also developed lines with external designers such as Moisés de la Renta, the son of one of the biggest names in international *haute couture*, Óscar de la Renta.

This strategy can also help companies extend their product catalogue at reduced research and development cost, since similar garments can be differentiated easily and simply with the signature of a celebrity on them.

Hiring popular personalities to sign or design a collection is a rising trend among companies in the sector, and there are many examples of this, for example Kate Moss for Longchamp and Chloë Sevigny for Opening Ceremony.

b) **Collaboration with celebrities who lend their image**

Traditionally, these personalities have lent their images to produce catalogues or advertising campaigns using some medium and/or communications channel, but lately the tendency has been to develop additional collaborative arrangements with the companies.

With a view to achieving greater media impact, the large companies are making use of the presence of big names at their most important events, such as their seasonal presentations, openings of new stores, product launches, the presentation of a new brand image, sponsorship of some relevant project, awarding of prizes or the organization of its competitions. The result is that it is now common to see very well-known personalities, and even more frequently bloggers, at the runways shows of different designers, since they are lending their image to a variety of brands. Mango, for example, frequently enhances its shows with the best known faces from society, film, fashion, music and television.

Another form of collaboration is to use publicity as opposed to conventional advertising. In these cases, the ambassadors of the brand represent it in a discrete way, showing off the garments at social or professional events. Mango also makes use of this resource when presenting its own fashion shows.

All these activities, now common among the companies in the sector, were already being organized by Mango in the 1990s, as noted in the previous chapter. Not only did they use these big names for advertising campaigns, the company worked with celebrities of this ilk for big corporate events, such as the El Botón-Mango Fashion Awards (which included couturiers of worldwide fame). Other famous faces associated with the brand are Scarlett Johansson, Lizzy Jagger, Dree Hemingway and Sophie Auster. Taking part in specific campaigns, such as those on the QuemepongobyMango. com site, we have seen actresses and models such as Eugenia Silva, Goya Toledo, Ariadne Artiles, Dakota Johnson, Dree Hemingway, Laura Ponte and Max Irons.

c) Other collaborative arrangements

There are any number of collaborative arrangements between opinion leaders and the famous with fashion companies. Apart from what we have described above, another common phenomenon is when an image is lent in solidarity for supporting social causes. An example of this is in the design of handbags with a social focus by Scarlett Johansson for Mango. Actress Belén Rueda presented her solidarity-aware designs for the *Menudos Corazones* [Little Hearts] Foundation, of which she is the Honorary President. Designer Hannibal Laguna created T-shirts to benefit the reconstruction of Haiti in the wake of last year's earthquake, and in concert with Shakira and UNICEF he has designed African-inspired T-shirts aimed at raising money to fund children's education initiatives in South Africa.

Sometimes brands turn their consumers into opinion leaders, for example, when they supply them with garments and then the consumers appear in the media, reinforcing the brand in the public's mind.

4. Tell me what you wear and I'll tell you who you are

There is no doubt that the brands use celebrities to impact their target public. But why do consumers attach value to the effect generated by the brand ambassadors when they make purchasing decisions?

Figure 5.2 Influence Effects Between Celebrities & Consumers.

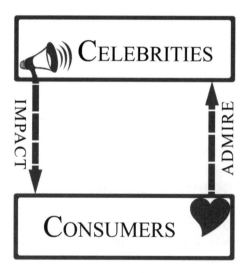

This is explained by Ángel Castiñeira, head of the Department of Social Sciences at ESADE and Doctor of Philosophy and Educational Sciences at the University of Barcelona: "Advertising audience leaders affect us from our pre-conscious stage, from when we are children. At that stage, our cultural and identity baggage is incomplete and shapes itself and develops in part by cultural identification processes."

Using this basic explanation, Castiñeira makes a distinction between the opinion leader and the audience leader according to the degree of impact they achieve. Hence, the opinion leader becomes a benchmark. He or she affects us when our level of awareness and maturity is already well developed, while the audience leader, associated more with advertising, affects us during our childhood. When we are adults we can partially distance ourselves from some of the cultural patterns we have received, but it cannot be denied that brands help define our identity.

If we accept that the definition of fashion is as a social phenomenon that is more important than clothing *per se,* we can go on to state that fashion meets needs which go beyond those which are merely physiological (except in the case of less developed countries) described by humanist psychologist Abraham Maslow (1908-1970).

Expert analysts like Grant McCracken claim that "clothing has moved away from a simple functional role to another that is wholly social, aesthetic and cultural. We use it to express cultural principles and social distances."

In other words, fashion satisfies a double need:

- It meets membership requirements, changing an individual into part of a group, which satisfies the need to belong to a social group;
- It fulfills needs for recognition and prestige, distinguishing an individual from the crowd and contributing personality.

On the one hand, we want our group to accept us, but we also seek identification with opinion and audience leaders; we follow their advice or imitate their behaviour patterns. They also help to satisfy the need for recognition, which is achieved by adopting certain features and behaviour patterns that distinguish us from others.

Although it may seem paradoxical, a purchaser who buys something is projecting a desire to reaffirm a different identity, and at the same time, a need for acceptance. In other words, the influence of the consumer is the outcome of a balance between the internal group (social) and the external group (opinion and audience leaders).

Figure 5.3 Influences on Consumers.

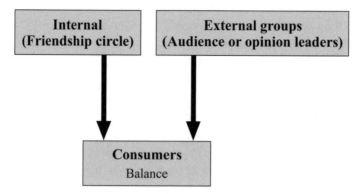

In Castiñeira's words, "human beings are community primates who configure and develop their incomplete cultural baggage during childhood. This identity is shaped by cultural immersion and cultural identification processes that shape the ego via personalities or brands."

The social need for membership is more pressing in childhood or adolescence, and brands play an important part during these stages. At these ages young people pursue their quest for identity and seeking stereotypes that identify them with various groups or urban tribes.

Figure 5.4 Examples of Urban Tribes & Icons.

METALLICA	The band Metallica is associated and identified with the urban tribe known as "heavy".
(peace sign)	The peace sign contributes to the hippie identity.
(Bob Marley)	Bob Marley and the colours yellow, red and green (the three colours of the Rastafarian flag) are associated with the Rastas.
(ska image)	Black and white checks are the pattern identified with the ska movement.
(roundel)	The logo based on the British Air Force roundel was associated with the London Mods in the 1960s.

As mentioned before, once a person reaches adulthood, they will continue to identify with personalities or brands, although the distance will be greater the more mature that person is.

Popular or famous personalities not only help buttress the personality of the purchaser, they also help build it. Every famous individual is associated with something because of their personality and the public identifies with them or not depending on their own character. Many people associate actress Angelina Jolie with solidarity, Rania of Jordan or Jacqueline Kennedy with elegance and Courtney Love or Agyness Deyn with rebellion and modernity, to offer some examples.

In reality, none of this is new. History tells us that fashion already served to satisfy the need to belong in the past. The development of fashion intensified after the French Revolution (at the end of the 18th century), when social classes were being shattered and social progress and the parts played by the people were multiplying. When mass production appeared later on (at the end of the 18th and beginning of the 19th centuries), it brought fashion to a much greater public and created new needs within that public, such as the need to be different, and it is from that time on that we can speak of the fashion market.

Apart from the social function played by the brands and the celebrities in the consumers' quest for identification, the emotional influence these people have on brands is also worth analyzing. From this point of view, Mango's collaboration with the most popular faces of the time has been successful in reaching the consumer not because of the product, but because of emotions and desires.

Mango headquarters – Barcelona.

Management of the entire company at world level is centralised at the general headquarters. This includes anything from a Human Resources-related job to solving problems to do with computer systems in the shops.

Mango believes in new technologies. A good example is the personnel reception plan which handles the way staff are instructed by the training department. This is designed to give new employees an understanding and general picture of the company as a whole. The reception programme consists of an on-line system which tells the newcomer about the history, values, culture, products, in-house services, organisational structure and the various departments. This aspect of the training scheme is rounded off with a guided tour through Mango's plant.

The *El Hangar* Design Centre is one of the biggest design centres in Europe. At the present time the workforce there is some 600-strong, a team whose brief is to produce innovative, creative and practical designs for the company's customers throughout the world. In other words, it means that it is here that the trends for the next Mango season are set, where the designs, fabrics and other materials are chosen for the new lines we shall be launching in the upcoming weeks. Practical and creative are the bywords of the philosophy behind the work of this space where we seek to develop new talent and the most streamlined communication channels between the various teams which are essential to a company of the size Mango.

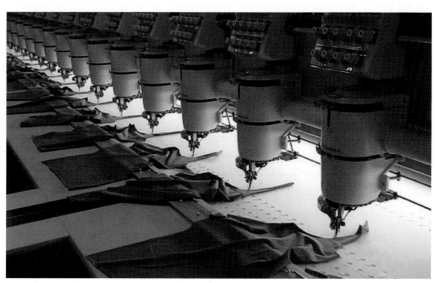

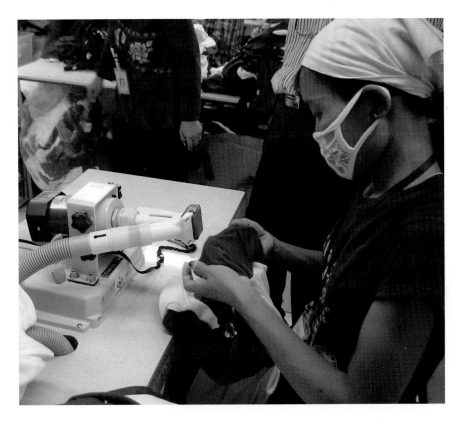

The importance of suppliers. A large number of companies are kept busy manufacturing and making up Mango products on a world-wide basis. Demands are at the highest level, because the brand's end-customers expect a very definite quality, although that by no means implies that they are indifferent to details of other kinds. The Corporate Social Responsibility policies ensure that all the garments and accessories manufactured by Mango are produced in keeping with the very strictest of controls as regards dimensions, installations and working methods, which must all comply with the Company code of conduct. Regular in-house and external audits are organised to ensure that suppliers fulfil these requirements. In many cases, the relationship with these suppliers has developed over years, and strong bonds exist between them. The quality lies in the product, naturally, but also in the manufacturing conditions and procedures, and in the health and safety standards protecting the workers.

"At Mango, we're all members of the logistics team," says Enric Casi, the company CEO, illustrating the importance of this heart which pumps the blood to keep the system working and never stopping. Mango logistics is fantastically complex because of the huge size of the company and the vast spread of points of sale. They have their own system – the Mango Logistics System – which the firm has developed over time, acquiring and adapting the latest technology at its installations, so that they can currently categorise and distribute thousands of garments in a hour. The system is an integrated logistical model based on speed, information and technology. It can handle information coming in from any corner of the world from any one of its almost 200 suppliers and keep up with orders coming in from over 1,700 points of sale, not to mention being ready to cope with a total in excess of 3,000 which are expected to come on stream in the upcoming decade.

And everything lies in customer service. Mango's true obsession lies in its points of sale. The aim is to build a brand which is easily recognisable and which seduces potential customers so that they really *fall in love* with Mango. The store is the place where the customer is guaranteed a 100% satisfactory purchasing experience, and where each and every tiny detail is taken care of.

6

Business Figures and Organizational Structure

The commercial company known as Mango is the property of Mango MNG Holding S.L., the group which includes all the various companies and locations where the principal activity is the design, distribution and marketing of articles of clothing and accessories by means of its distribution chain.

The Catalan firm closed the 2009 financial year with a turnover of 1,480 million Euros, a 2.8 per cent rise from the previous year, when sales were worth 1,440 million. The company's turnover was 78 per cent from foreign markets, one point greater than in 2008, while the Spanish market stood at 22 per cent. In addition to this, turnover for goods sold on the internet reached 11.7 million Euros, a figure likely to grow in 2010 with the opening of shops in Russia and China.

During the 2009 financial year, the company opened 161 new shops, 153 of which were located outside of Spain, and which included new markets such as Iran, Belarus and Guatemala.

For 2010, the company is predicting an investment of 100 million Euros for new shops, shop redesigns and the application of new logistical systems. Plans are also afoot to consolidate the European market with a reinforced presence in Germany, Austria, Italy, the Netherlands, Belgium, France, Sweden, Switzerland and the UK. As for the market on the American continent, there are great hopes for new points of sale in Chile, Peru and Mexico.

With a view to maintaining the high growth rate in foreign markets, plans are underway to make an initial entry into the islands of Mauritius and New Caledonia, plus open new shops in cities such as Bogota, Caracas, Dubai, Paris, Moscow, Beijing and Rabat, among others.

For Mango, the biggest stake continues to be in China, where it hopes to open 59 points of sale, as well as buttress its presence in other Asian markets such as South Korea, Singapore and India, where there is a shop at the New Delhi airport.

Despite the soundness and high level of development of the Mango project over recent years, Enric Casi says that the international crisis is bound to affect turnover forecasts for 2010, although data are yet to be consolidated at the time of closing this book.

In 2009 Spain, the USA, the UK and Ireland were the countries worst hit by reduced activity, but even in 2010, improvement was detected. In any case, overall figures are offset by positive results from other countries.

For Isak Andic, "the best antidote to the crisis is globalization, and that means more than just an export-focused approach." In actual fact, the medium term objective is for Spain to represent a mere 10 per cent of total group turnover.

Despite the difficulties of the current situation, Mango is sticking by its forecast to continue to open between 150 and 200 points of sale annually, and to stake more on emerging markets such as China, Russia or Mexico, notwithstanding consolidation in Europe. The fact is, claims Andic, the business he founded is only just beginning to expand abroad, and so far no limits have been set, since the business has a presence on only 30 per cent of the main shopping streets worldwide.

If we make a sales growth comparison, we see that in 2003, turnover from the company's own shops stood at 423,836 million Euros, while in 2009 the figure reached was 684 million. The positive differential is also seen in the sales through franchises, which invoiced 346,978 million in 2003 and rose to 460,428 in 2009. Over the 2009-2012 period, the aim is to increase turnover by 15 per cent annually from all the shops as a whole (a forecast which is so far being achieved).

Of the total business volume, 78 per cent of sales are in foreign markets. Mango is already present in over 100 countries with 1,400 shops, and the goal is to double this figure to some 3,000 shops in the next few years. In the meantime, the target for 2011 is a total of 2,300 points of sale. In that year there will be a "before and after" situation, because the conviction at the head office is that a very big change will take place in turnover and production development. This forecast is also closely linked to business at points of sale in shopping centres, where bigger crowds gather. This business model and the growth forecasts are explained in greater detail in the chapter on franchises.

New technologies also play an important part in this growth, since it is thanks to them that it is possible to reinforce and boost a higher level of integration and collaboration between suppliers, manufacturers, websites, logistics operators, points of sale and the head office.

At the end of 2009, the payroll stood at 8,600 people, 1,800 of whom were based at the head office in Palau-solità i Plegamans, a building which covers an area of 164,000 square metres.

The size of these figures reveals that we are talking about a successful brand and model, not just because of its understanding of fashion and capacity for trend-setting, but also for its belief in, and commitment to, a business model from which the company has grown steadily and uninterruptedly for the past 26 years.

1. Structure of the organization and corporate control

Mango is a family group with two major shareholders: Isak Andic, president, and Nahman Andic, vice-president. Both not only control management, but take a direct part in it, and communications between all areas of the business is complete and ongoing at all levels. In other words, it is evident that Mango is a multinational group with a family character, both as regards ownership and management.

The Board of Directors consists of the aforementioned shareholders, five other directors who are minority shareholders and executive directors who have trained in the company and have experience in the sector. These directors are Enric Casi, (CEO), Nicolás Olivé (head of Corporate Social Responsibility, building maintenance and management of the shops), Salvador Vallés (design, purchasing, production and quality control), Daniel López (licenses and agreements with other brand and co-branding, communications, real-estate management and franchisee care), Damián Sánchez (creative director) and Isak Halfon (expansion manager).

And lastly, in the general management area, Casi has a range of responsibilities in logistics; HR and organization; legal/auditing; information systems and new technologies; operations and e-business. At the same time, each of the areas described is delegated to an executive responsible for management who reports to his superiors.

The members of the Board of Directors are the only shareholders in the group, and their remuneration, as with the members of the executive committee, consists of a fixed portion and a variable portion depending upon the financial objectives achieved.

The operational structure is divided into two levels: the members of the Board of Directors and the managers on the executive committee. Top leadership falls to the president of the company, who also takes on a range of functions and executive jobs.

In 2008, an executive committee was set up consisting of the members of the Board of Directors and eight other people, also professionally trained in the group's companies.

In an extremely competitive world such as fashion, Mango has been able to reinvent itself and remain true to its principles, thanks to an ethical and sustainable management model that includes a series of in-house controls assessed by the Board of Directors and the Executive

Committee and undertaken in collaboration with the Internal Inspection and CSR departments. They analyze all possible risks in order to take the necessary measures to tackle a situation.

On a regular basis, the Board and the Committee also evaluate the most suitable financial strategy for the company, making decisions for investments on the basis of criteria concerned with profitability and opportunity, and making the necessary present and future adjustments.

The Mango group has an in-house auditing department that is responsible for a continuous assessment of the areas of the organization. This department reports directly to the general management and the group directors.

Figure 6.1 Company Flow Chart.

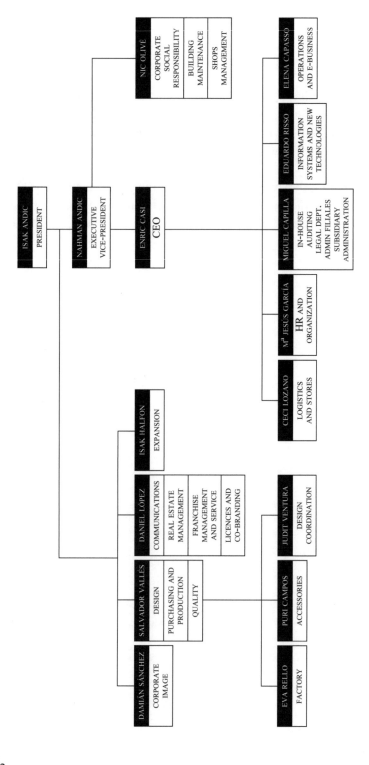

Source: Mango annual report 2009.

7

A Unique Management Model

The computerized logistics centre located in Parets del Vallés (Barcelona) is one of Mango's dreams come true. The dynamic distribution centre equipped with the latest technology in this field, has an area of 24,000 square metres and specializes in the distribution of folded garments. The head office, which previously handled folded garments, now deals exclusively with hanging garments. The logistics centre began operations in November 2008, but as the managers say, it was not until two years later that it began to operate with the anticipated output.

At this centre, all processes are automated: loading, warehousing, invoicing and dispatching. In this way the effort required from the staff is kept to a minimum and their work input is optimized.

Investment from the point of view of engineering began in 1988. At that time, the company had thirteen points of sale in Spain and was involved in upgrading the warehouse management system along with logistics and product distribution management. It was at that time that the production system, based on the just-in-time distribution policy, began to develop and concepts regarding product, shop interior design, quality, price and brand image began to be defined. It was this solid foundation among other factors which supported its leadership in the textiles sector. The just-in-time model is a management system whereby it is easier to match stock to demand.

To streamline this policy to match the volume of its shops, Mango spent years working on its logistics system, until finally, in 2000, it achieved a personalized operational model, whereby it was possible to classify and distribute 30,000 garments per hour.

Mango's logistics system is based on speed, information and technology. The goal is to ensure that each of its points of sale will at any moment have the stock it needs, according to turnover and garment supply. With a production of 90 million garments per year, this system guarantees constant turnaround and production adjusted to the rate required by demand, both in terms of volume and speed.

At the present moment two different production systems exist, known in-house as manufacturers and production workshops. The manufacturers receive the product patterns designed by the company and take responsibility for making them up and for buying the raw materials prior to production. When the product is ready it is dispatched to Mango. The production workshops also receive the patterns and produce the garments, but unlike the manufacturers, it is Mango that takes responsibility for buying the raw materials used to make the garment, and for sending them to the suppliers to be made.

Whether one system or the other is more convenient depends basically on geography (proximity) and technical factors (according to how specialized production is). In financial year 2009, 71 per cent of production was handled by the manufacturers and 20 per cent by the production workshops. The volume of garments and accessories manufactured over the same period reached approximately 85 million units.

Regardless of who handles the production process, it must still be undertaken in keeping with company codes, and to ensure that this is the case, quality control inspections are carried out and the firm must adhere to Mango's Code of Conduct, as defined in the CSR policy. Almost as though it was a declaration of human rights, relationships with suppliers are established by taking a long-term view (in some cases, this commercial bond has been in place for up to, or even more than, 20 years) as are their sustainable commitments. A system based on joint planning and work is established between Mango and its suppliers, involving direct technical support at their production centres.

This demonstrates mutual trust at the level of sustainable commitment and efficiency on both sides, indispensable when it comes to defining all the processes, from design to direct sale to the consumer in any part of the world and for ensuring that medium-high quality is maintained.

In any case, the company has no direct or indirect holding in the business of any manufacturer or production workshop producing its products. Furthermore, none of these manufacturers or workshops operate exclusively for Mango who make use of some 200 suppliers and indirectly employ 23,000 people.

All the garments and accessories are designed in accordance with general collection guidelines, for which production and distribution planning is crucial. Clear quality criteria are also established to cover the entire process, and are monitored from beginning to end.

Responsibility for the development of a garment's pattern falls directly on the manufacturer or production workshop, except in occasional cases where it is limited by legislation on grounds of origin or quota. The manufacturing period lasts an average of three or four months from the time an order is received, although this period may be less, depending upon various factors (raw material stocks, etc.). Dispatches to the stores are planned before each season and production is organized in accordance with this criterion. If sales forecasts are not met, the balance between dispatches or exchanges between stores is organized by the warehouse and by Mango's head office. Then the remainder of the season's garments are marketed via discounts and promotions.

During the 2009 financial period, Mango worked with 194 garment manufacturers and 326 accessory workshops worldwide. As regards purchase quota per country, the largest was China, with 39.7%; in Morocco 26.7% of the production was done; Turkey produced 12.7%; Vietnam, 7.3%; India, 5.6%; Indonesia, 3%; Pakistan, 2.8% and Bangladesh did 1%. The remaining 1.2% was shared between a selection of countries.

Suppliers are free to manufacture their products in more than one factory, alternate them over time according to the technical characteristics of the product and vary them on occasion, in line with this criterion.

In terms of logistics, Mango uses the system known as cross-docking, which refers to a type of order preparation in which articles are neither placed in a warehouse nor picked up. This system makes it possible to transfer materials to different destinations or consolidate merchandise from different sources without intermediate warehousing, which cuts the time of logistical operations. The final goal is to reduce the costs of delivery, warehousing and preparation. Another advantage of the system is automatic garment classification using conveyor belts. Orders for approximately 20 per cent of production in 2008 were handled using this model.

To achieve efficiency, close, continual communication and collaboration with suppliers, logistics operators and shops is necessary, and for this reason the company has set up a product development ICT platform whereby it is possible to send and receive information according to the needs of each user. This platform also makes it possible to monitor the entire supply chain.

The control policy and production characteristics mean that both manufacturers and production workshops cannot unilaterally subcontract the manufacture of the garments. Only in those cases where it is essential can they outsource production to a third company, but this must be with the knowledge and prior authorization of Mango.

Despite the fact that all the suppliers have verticalized the production process (cutting, producing, pressing, packaging, etc), on occasions there are requirements for special processes that they cannot handle (embroidery, for example) and on these occasions, they outsource to third parties. When third-party production reaches a certain volume, these companies also become part of the control and monitoring system organized by the company. This explains the fact that every season new suppliers are incorporated into the whole to tackle technical requirements and production increases.

All companies are required to meet requirements for all details. As far as finished products are concerned, for example, Mango distributes written instructions to the suppliers regarding the standards governing the use of products and substances involved in manufacturing. Once the production process has begun, these substances are checked by means of an exhaustive analysis of all the articles.

This checking procedure involves selecting certain garments or accessories from each reference group according to established statistical criteria and sending them to the laboratory for full analysis and subsequent issue of a certificate for all articles.

In this system, the selection of reference items for analysis always takes the garments and accessories from the final production run, since changes might occur in the fabrics and their components, as well as in the materials acquired by the supplier during the design process and initial production tests.

The instructions for suppliers include lists of materials that are regulated by the laws of various countries as well as those that are not. Monitoring and control of all materials is undertaken in line with specific statistical criteria.

Guaranteeing dispatch to the stores and maintaining consistent quality calls for very sophisticated technological implementation. In actual fact, as we have already mentioned, these new technologies are some of the most important strategic tools used by the company. By means of an in-house corporate portal, built into the company intranet that is the gateway to all its information systems, Mango coordinates each and every one of the processes that form the production and distribution chain.

Information is managed by means of an ICT platform which offers centralized access to corporate, commercial and employment information, not to mention information regarding relationships with suppliers. This is actually a shared connection known as B2E, Business to Employees, designed to achieve an increase in productivity, and also optimize the image the employees themselves have of the company where they work.

With its company-wide intranet, Mango also manages its in-house image with a communications policy that keeps employees informed about everything concerning the company, supplies them with corporate and in-house news, and offers an advertising board, areas for surveys and enquiries, discussion forums where they can express their ideas, a suggestion box and the company directory. This connectivity-based relationship also extends to the Human Resources area, which provides employees with the in-house network for organizing time off, and for checking their work schedules and social benefits.

General services communicate resource and room reservation systems, information regarding work hazards or the environment, and there is a section for offering and requesting services. It is important to point out that this portal is adapted to the needs and specific nature of each of the countries in which Mango operates.

In addition to all these services, the house network creates a relationship framework between suppliers and points of sale. At the pre-production or final test stages, the company has a co-produced platform for product development that helps suppliers access all the information on a product from the very moment when the design was presented.

At the same timeand in the process of implementation is a program that will monitor, track and support production. Suppliers will be provided with an ICT tool that will show them, at any time, all the details of the general procedures, such as the planning for the season.

In general terms, this will be an interactive, two-way tool that will open the door to all kinds of consultations and comments. Setting up this technological development that facilitates an information exchange with suppliers, distributors and factories was rendered particularly complex because of the multiplicity of questions arising from the technical and ICT sectors, which cast its very viability in doubt; although all doubts were finally overcome.

This situation was resolved by motivating and rewarding innovation via financial benefits, the traditional system used by vendors. And in this case, innovation was associated with pressure and overcoming barriers. For example, it was necessary to coincide with the timetables of other countries that called for work to be done in real time with

American logistics operators. In the end, this helped to develop the project even more quickly, but it still took three years for the successful completion of its integration.

At Mango, innovation is approached by teamwork, by using the resources available on the internet, the intranet and by other means. At regular intervals suppliers pay visits to the head office in order to strengthen contacts, and this gives them an opportunity to analyze the various aspects of production and business in general from a closer perspective. These personal contacts complement the technical support provided by the quality control teams that are constantly available at their premises.

Another work space is the Hangar Design Center, thought to be the biggest of its kind in Europe. It is located in Palau-solità i Plegamans (Barcelona) and commenced its operations in 2006. It occupies an area of 12,000 square metres and is staffed by over 600 professionals in the field of women's fashions and accessories. Rather than establishing design centres at different locations throughout the world, the company decided to concentrate the entire project within a single space where individuals from over thirty different nationalities could interconnect. This centre includes sections for design, purchasing and quality, and the employees work in teams. The average age of the people working here is under 31. Almost 87 per cent are women. In terms of the design, the Hangar was built on the structure of a former factory, and has been perfectly adapted for its new use and purpose. The building was designed on the basis of ecologically efficient principles, including electronic temperature regulation, closed-circuit air-conditioning and optimal use of natural light.

Additionally, Mango operates its own classification and packing system using a unique computer system to optimize the contents of the cases that are dispatched from the distribution centres to the shops, so that their spatial capacity is used to best advantage.

In the case of hanging garments, cases are not used for transportation from the production centre to the distribution centre, regardless of the transport type used. And cases are no longer used for merchandise distributed to the stores by road.

1. Product dispatch

The manufacture and receipt of finished goods by the suppliers is always consolidated in each production area and dispatched, practically in its totality, in full containers by sea.

In neighbouring countries where production takes place and seaborne transportation is not an option, goods travel by road. But in countries and regions where the stores are located and the use of such a system is possible, manufactured goods are distributed to the shops by bunching them for the country in question directly with the rest of the products manufactured in other areas, thereby avoiding unnecessary transport.

Deliveries to shops are made from the various warehouses via completely optimized cargo deliveries, andgarments and accessories are restocked at regular intervals, depending on sales. However, the first deliveries of the season's stock are carried out, whenever possible, using the merchandise transfer in transit system.

2. Activity centres

Organizational activities are carried out in a series of the company's own installations, located at the central head office in Palau-solità y Plegamans (warehouse and offices) and at two warehouses located in the vicinity of the head office, in Montcada i Reixac y Terrassa, as well as via various of its own shops and franchises. The company leases six more warehouse complexes, located in Parets, Montornés and Sabadell (Barcelona), and in the cities of Shenzhen and Hong Kong (in China) and New Jersey (in the USA).

In 2007, a new warehouse began operations in the community of Sallent (Barcelona) where the entire management of the materials sent to shops (consumables such as bags and hangers, interior furniture, advertising and display equipment) is centralized. The work at this warehouse includes checking and receiving garment deliveries returned by shops, whether for alterations or because the season ended, and there the garments will be reassessed and selected for return to the sales channel.

In 2008, a new, fully computerized, logistics centre located in Parets del Vallés, began operations using the latest technologies, that as mentioned before, made it possible to considerably upgrade distribution capacity. This plant was designed to blend in with its surrounding environment in order to minimize its visual impact.

3. New projects: Mango's logistics city

The logistics city is a project that is currently in the construction stage. It will cover an area equivalent to 120 football pitches. It is located in the Barcelona suburb of Lliçà and the company has had to wait 10 years for this area to be re-zoned for industrial use. At last, and after a great deal of bureaucratic wrangling and permit issue delays, 75% of the entire area (300,000 square metres) will be zoned for industrial use while the remaining 25% must be used for tertiary purposes.

On this second commercial block, 10,000 square metres will be used to market seasonal remainders and surpluses; companies other than Mango will also be permitted to establish themselves here. For the remainder of the commercial area a promoter partner who specializes in leisure centres will be sought to take charge of building hotels and entertainment areas, among other projects. Mango will only be responsible for promoting and organizing the industrial zone, the area destined for the brand's future logistics city.

With the creation of this city, Mango will have a much larger logistics and distribution centre than where it currently operates, which will also be one of the most advanced in the world. The textile company will be investing 360 million Euros in the industrial zone over the next eight years, and it is expected that it will be developed within around five years. Within six years, according to predictions, the building intended for all the hanging garments will be ready. After this, folded garments, currently located at the Parets del Vallès centre, will be transferred there.

The thinking behind this monumental infrastructure is Mango's perception of the world as a single market; at least, so we are assured by CEO Enric Casi when he describes and explains his model of worldwide production and distribution.

In summation, the single management office in Palau-solità i Plegamans, and the logistics and warehousing department, form Mango's operational centre for any country or city. An illustration of the situation would be the case of the United Kingdom, where, although there are 700 staff there is no office. Until fairly recently Mango had a logistics centre in the United Arab Emirates, but in the end it was dismantled when it was realized that operations were much more manageable if control was retained from a central location. The distribution ratio consists of daily services to European stores compared with two order services per week for the rest of the world. The sole exception is for China, where for administrative purposes, Mango still maintains an open warehouse for handling local needs.

8

Franchising as a Model for Expansion and Growth

The beginning of the 1990s marked a crucial change in the Mango strategy. At that time it appeared that the organization was set to grow exponentially, and to cope with this a series of changes were set in place to make this growth possible, the most important of all being to base the business on a mixed model of franchise and its own shops.

Franchising is an expansion model that has been in action in our country for over 30 years, consisting of a commercial relationship based on a company (the franchisor) that transfers the business of operating a group of industrial or intellectual property rights, brands, commercial names, logos, models, author's rights, etc., to another company (the franchisee), in return for a consideration (royalty), for the sale of products or the provision of services.

This business model has undergone considerable growth throughout the world and is well established in Spain. At the present moment, franchises can be found in practically every sector, but the most popular ones using this business model are in the areas of beauty and cosmetics, specialist shops and textiles/home furnishings.

The crisis does not seem to have put an end to this growth model, according to the Spanish Franchisees' Association (AEF) report on 31 December, 2009 saying that franchises existed for 919 chains, covering 57,139 businesses, a 5 per cent increase over the previous year.

Regarding the level of women's fashion companies represented, the number of names has fallen over the past year from 59 to 48. Nevertheless, as we show below, there is no shortage of companies going in for this system.

To make a comparison between Mango and other large brands that have opted to expand via franchises, below we have shown some of the companies from a range of sectors, particularly fashion, who have chosen this model. Although these are just a few examples, we can see that this expansion formula is not a traditional illustration for fashion businesses aimed at the general public. Indeed, Mango's main competitors, H&M and Inditex, have distanced themselves in this respect and prefer to own their own shops.

Figure 8.1 Principal Spanish Fashion Brands with Franchises.

Sector	Company	Sector	Company
Fashion	Mango	Accessories	Aïta
Fashion	Benetton	Children's products	Chicco
Fashion	Adolfo Domínguez	Children's fashion	Bóboli
Women's fashion	Kookai	Underwear	Intimissimi
Women's fashion	Custo Barcelona	Underwear	Women'secret
Women's fashion	Etxart & Panno	Underwear	Calzedonia
Men's fashion	Celio	Underwear	Etam

The franchise system allows a company to expand quickly and penetrate markets that might be more complex as regards administration and management. It is important to point out that the success of a franchise depends to a large extent on a consistent and homogeneous image, as it is this which is marketed through the shops.

Mango decided to opt for the franchising system to globalize the company in 1992, when Isak Andic decided that they needed an international presence and that the business should expand worldwide.

Given that franchises must adapt locally, even though they are based on a global model, that year Andic decided to launch the business in neighbouring countries Portugal and France, which happened two years later (1994). When the first successes were established, the company made itself known abroad at the International Franchise Salon in Paris in 1996. The outcome of this was the opening of the first shops in Germany.

Since then, the company has 807 shops (2009) that have adopted this operating system, which represents 58 per cent of the total number of stores. Thanks to them, Mango has a presence throughout the entire European Union and in the major cities of the world. The fact that more than half of the shops are franchises shows how important the system is to the company's expansion and growth model. In actual fact, at the present moment Mango's strategy is to open their own shops only if the city is particularly significant or the shops will be on a large scale.

The Mango franchise system provides the franchisee with an integrated raft of services that support all aspects of merchandising the product and managing the business. It also offers shop layouts, window displays, product selection and advertising. The franchisee must provide human resources management, and will be required to pay the staff a higher wage than the market average with a view to increasing the employees' satisfaction level. The franchisee must also take charge of leasing or buying the premises, and may operate more than one shop (in actual fact, only seven people control the brand's shops in Portugal).

Figure 8.2 Percentage of Own Stores versus Franchise Stores.

Shops	1999	2000	2001	2002	2003	2004	2005	2006	2007	2008	2009
Franchises	288	290	330	392	462	522	605	682	713	739	807
%	62%	56%	57%	62%	66%	68%	70%	69%	65%	60%	58%
Own shops	175	225	245	237	242	246	261	313	381	489	583
%	38%	44%	43%	38%	34%	32%	30%	31%	35%	40%	42%
Total	463	515	575	629	704	768	866	995	1.094	1.228	1.390

Source: Sustainability report 2008.

Depending on the country, different economic conditions apply to the franchisees, which may vary between 40 per cent and 50 per cent of the margin, on top of the franchise market conditions in the fashion sector. Contracts are renewed on a yearly basis.

As with all systems of this kind, Mango insists on the strictest conditions covering the establishment of a franchise. Even so, according to Isak Halfon, Brand Expansion Manager, "the company has always looked for franchisees that are strongly committed to the business and identify with the brand." In his opinion, "the dedication needed to make the business work and the love of the brand itself, are as important as the capital to open a new business."

Over time, the basic conditions established for the franchisees have remained in place with the exception of the minimum space size required. In 2004, the minimum area was set at 700 square metres, while now it stands at 300. This change is explained by Enric Casi: "Before the crisis we had to free up some conditions in order to overcome some of the barriers the market imposed while still retaining the growth model."

1. Franchise Conditions

- Premises:
  - Located on the main street or in a shopping centre.
  - Minimum population of the city's nucleus of 80,000 people.
  - Interior design exclusively planned by Mango.

- Financial conditions. Entrance rights include:
  - Availability of a team in the fields of merchandising, display, ICT, stock organization and staff training that will support the opening.
  - Ongoing presence of a supervisor.

- Sale-or-return system:
  - Mango supplies the franchisees with sale-or-return stock. This means that the franchisee only pays a percentage of

the sale price, and the remainder is returned at the end of the season.

- o Shops on sale-or-return are connected to Mango via a communications system that supplies them with updated information about the stock of each shop.
- o Mango automatically replaces the sale-or-return stock at the shops each day in line with sales.
- o Consignments to shops on the sale-or-return basis continually include new articles, allowing for greater product turnover.
- o Goods are guaranteed via a bank guarantee.

- Shop design:
  - o Interior design layout and materials (approximately 700 Euros per square metre, civil engineering not included).
  - o Advertising and Public Relations (Communications): undertaken and planned by Mango, assessed at 4 per cent of total turnover.

The estimated minimum total investment to open a Mango franchise is around 500,000 Euros.

2. Adaptability and franchise management

Initially the franchisees had to buy the products as a firm purchase, but it was soon realized that it was better to offer the products on a sale-or-return basis. This would mean that the franchisee would only invoice the garments sold and would retain the ability to return product overstock. In other words, the Mango head office makes the decision about which garments are to be sent to the shops and controls the logistics. The head office also makes the decision about replacing products when sales are lower than expected.

The team of display artists, merchandisers, coordinators and supervisors ensures that each and every one of the points of sale shares the same ambience, offers a high level of attention to customers and is managed in the same way.

The franchise operating system is not repeated in every country with guaranteed success. In order to consolidate success, a detailed study of the environment is required and this means that the original model must be adapted to the region where the new shop is located. The franchisee must take great care to run the business in close compliance with the franchisee manual with an understanding of the development of the sector in which the shop is competing. Additionally, the franchisee must implement such changes as are appropriate to the business model so that the necessary innovations for remaining abreast of customers' habits (adaptation of sales techniques, appearance of new products, modification of certain aspects of corporate identity, etc.) are incorporated.

3. The relationship between Mango and its franchisees

Mango is a sale chain with the main aim of occupying sector leadership. Its dependency on an extensive network of franchises means that the management of the business is to a certain extent shared with its partners. This means that a permanent relationship exists in which the franchisees participate in different areas of the company to contribute their point of view.

In order to achieve excellence as far as the relationship and the management of both sides is concerned, the textiles company employs a trained team of supervisors, coordinators and country managers who visit the shops in their zones on a regular basis. Each supervisor is responsible for ten shops and visits them personally to make sure of the correct provision of all elements involved, as well as appropriate customer treatment. The supervisors report to their coordinator who manages a specific region or zone, and who in turn works under someone who controls a specific country or number of countries, depending on the number of shops.

When a new season opens, Mango holds a show for the franchisees in Palau-solità i Plegamans. During these occasions, various working sessions are organized to jointly analyze and decide what the most suitable garments and accessories will be for their shops according to the areas where they are located.

Mango is provided with specialist departments to support the expansion team, whomaintain ongoing relationships among themselves.

Xavier Carbonell, Head of Corporate Social Responsibility, states that "the franchisees also abide by the Code of Ethics because the contract they sign includes this agreement. Regular audits are also carried out."

4. Growth strategy via corners in department stores

One of the expansion strategies with great potential for the textiles business is the shop known as a 'corner' located within the large department stores. The stores in question are very large in size and can depend on a tremendous number of people passing through.

At the present moment some 90 points of sale have been opened on a trial basis, but the plan is to open over 300 in 2010 worldwide, mainly in the United Arab Emirates and China. In the case of Europe, the key markets are France, Italy, Germany, the UK and Russia.

The management of the company is convinced that these spaces in particular will be the cornerstone of growth in the years to come, but at the present time Enric Casi acknowledges that they are in a learning curve, discovering what would work best for turnover. One of the areas currently being analzsed is how products should be adapted to potential buyers and what the restocking rate should be.

To this range of commercial channels should be added the traditional points of sale, which will maintain the planned level of opening and development of the shops specifically for men (HE) and accessories (Mango Touch).

9

A Responsible and Sustainable Approach

There is no doubt that Mango is a company with a great vocation for social action and very clearly defined ethical principles. A good example would be its compliance with the Code of Conduct that it has established for its suppliers. In this sense, the actual production and quality system determine the specific profile of the supplier and specific characteristics for the factories with a view to avoiding the risk of non-compliance.

This relationship is typified and regulated in the company Corporate Social Responsibility policy which lays down various requirements and very clear standards that the suppliers must meet, as well as Mango's responsibilities towards its suppliers. This policy has its repercussions on the global projection of the brand and on the way consumers and the competition perceive it. In today's world, consumers buy not only design or function when they acquire a product; they are also concerned with the brand's intangible values, and will reject, for example, brands whose behaviour is less than ethical when it comes to choosing suppliers.

From the corporate point of view, the CSR responds to a model for suppliers and employees, who see a model to follow in the company and experience a feeling of pride to be a part of it, or work with it.

Goals of this type would be impossible without a firm consensus on the part of a management team that made CSR a present and future commitment and a work philosophy that matched the entrepreneurial spirit.

As with every company, Mango also nurtures the utopian dream of improving the world in which we live. In no case is this an attitude dreamed up on the run to chime with politically correct management styles; rather, we are witnessing the company's continual efforts to seek opportunities for applying its philosophies in all kinds of details, including the involvement of third parties.

To implement this, a Code of Ethics has been shaped with fundamental benchmark values and principles that allow business goals to be achieved through a blend of enthusiasm, creativity and continuous training.

The foundations on which the Mango philosophy are built are harmony (as opposed to conflict), humility (as opposed to high-handedness, arrogance and pride), and affection (as opposed to indifference and resentment). Other equally relevant values must be factored in as complements to those values, such as:

- o honesty and mutual respect,
- o perseverance,
- o responsibility and a spirit of cooperation,
- o keenness to learn and continually improve,
- o innovation and creativity,
- o team work and shared objectives,
- o satisfaction and enthusiasm for a job well done,
- o seeing changes as opportunities and not threats,
- o the simplification of tasks and minimization of bureaucracy,
- o and finally, leading by example.

The ethical principles of the Mango group also include a commitment to undertake all business operations and activities within the framework of an appropriate and reasonable moral attitude applied to all business decisions and operations, and always undertaken within the law.

All the brand's franchisees are contractually bound to comply with this Code of Ethics. A specific Code of Conduct matching the company Code of Ethics and also contractually binding for the manufacturers and production workshops has also been developed.

Mango likewise makes purchases that offer standardization regarding the excellence of all its products, guaranteeing that none imply risks to the customer's health and safety.

The Code of Ethics must be obeyed, both individually as well as by the entire collective, via teamwork. Anybody who visits the company and becomes familiar with Mango's approach and philosophy immediately perceives that people seek to do things well in this environment, where the rules are clear and defined according to standards that are strictly followed. It may be for this reason that financial profitability is established over the long term and is not a priority in every decision taken.

Isak Andic and his management team have always worked with a strategic view based on a broad panorama; the idea that the company, established in the 1970s, would make its mark on the fashion world through its advanced approach compared to the rest of its competitor companies. There is no doubt that this kind of thinking is a driving force for the people who become part of the organization, including those working in indirect processes through the suppliers.

All aspects of the values specified that we have looked at previously are also incorporated into the group Corporate Social Responsibility policy. As Enric Casi puts it, "We want Mango to become a global benchmark for fashion because of its CSR policies."

We can distinguish between two stages in the implementation of the totality of the CSR policies. Stage one covers the period from 1984-2000, and the second stage covers from 2001 to the present. In the initial period, a written commitment was given by the manufacturers and production workshops stating that they would abide by a series of social, labour and environmental standards. All were set down in a document that also specified general instructions for compliance.

Collaboration has also started on a series of social action projects that mainly consist of aid for occasional international emergency situations, agreements with various organizations to provide clothing, and campaigns for various causes (health, wellbeing, etc.).

On the environmental front, during the 1999 financial period a best practice programme was launched and in 2001 an environmental diagnostic study was carried out that became the starting point for all subsequent development in this area.

Stage two (2001-present) features a reinforcement of all the CSR aspects of the organisation. In November 2001, an agreement was signed whereby a single top-level European laboratory, the Technological Institute (AITEX), would guarantee that the garments and accessories contain no substances classified as hazardous to health.

In 2002, contacts and discussions with the parties concerned were opened. In February of that same year an agreement was signed with the NGO SETEM (the Spain coordinator of the Clean Clothes Campaign) designed to create a framework of cooperation and transparency making it possible to advance and consolidate various CSR aspects. The Corporate Social Responsibility department was also created with the job of establishing and coordinating CSR's policies and actions within the organization.

That same year Mango signed a world pact promoted by the United Nations (The Global Compact) that called on businesses to adopt ten universal principles in the fields of Human Rights, labour standards, the environment and the elimination of corruption. This pact was announced by the United Nations Secretary General, Kofi Annan, at the Davos World Economic Forum in January 1999, and it brought together businesses, employee associations and non-governmental organizations with the United Nations and other authorities to encourage collaboration and create a fairer global framework where all could participate. From the time of the signing of the pact an annual progress report has been drawn up regarding the various principles established in the pact.

In 2002, the policies and objectives of the organization were also outlined in a Code of Ethics, and the international benchmark standards and the principles and philosophy of the United Nations world pact were incorporated into various aspects of the CSR. This code laid down five impressive commitments relating to economics, society and labour, the environment, cooperation with society, and the quality and safety of the products.

This Code of Ethics was the reference used for the development, drafting and implementation of the June 2002 Code of Conduct that was binding for suppliers and that includes the applicable International Labour Organization (ILO) agreements and recommendations.

Since 2006, collaboration has been upgraded with the labour union, in specific terms with the Textiles and Chemical Federation (FITEQA), on matters such as the structure and content of the sustainability report, the randomly performed follow-up and verification of the company's own plant, and various factories with which Mango works.

In September 2006 an agreement was signed with the International Higher School of Business (ESCI), part of Pompeu Fabra University (UPF), to set up the Mango Chair of Corporate Social Responsibility, an initiative dedicated to stimulating research into various CSR areas at the international level.

In the university and business areas, Mango is involved in two specialist courses. Mango runs the first one, dealing with retail operations and focusing on management at the point of sale, in concert with ESCI.. The second, organized in collaboration with the Higher School of Design (ESDI), is a programme that deals with management in the fashion and design industry and covers matters concerned with the creation of a collection and the management of everything associated with it.

In 2007, Mango participated for the first time in the Multi-Fibre Agreement, MFA, a forum that promotes dialogue, collaboration and joint involvement among various organizations (companies, public institutions and social organizations) with the aim of promoting CSR throughout the production areas of the textiles sector, particularly as far as employees and local communities are concerned.

In 2009, contacts were opened with the Ecology and Development Foundation (ECODES) with a view to pressing forward in all aspects of policy, monitoring and follow-up on greenhouse gas emissions created by the company. The contacts in question were established in 2010, and in May of the same year ECODES performed a range of tests to calculate Mango's greenhouse gas emissions (step one). The result is ECODES' issue of the $ZeroCO_2$ accreditation label, confirming the organization's commitment in this area.

In June 2010, Mango was granted Made in Green certification. This certification, authorized by the Technological Textile Institute (AITEX), is a guarantee that none of its garments and accessories contain hazardous chemicals in keeping with the highest standards of the international market, and that all are manufactured in production centres with adequate environmental management systems and in accordance with employees' human and universal rights.

1. Relationships with the suppliers

The commercial relationship between Mango and some of its suppliers has developed over the long term, thanks to a sustainable commitment by all parties. This close relationship exists thanks to the intangible values represented by the brand and the trust that its international recognition implies, and above all, because loyalty among these parties is based on clearly defined commitments and considerations.

In order for the management systems of a company that designs, manufactures, distributes and markets fashion textile products and accessories to constantly perform, it is essential that the entire chain of communicatonis smoothly articulated and that relationships function reciprocally in terms of quality and efficiency. The number of clothing garment suppliers rose in 2009 to a total of 129.

Code of Conduct for manufacturers and production workshops

As we have seen, Mango set up an obligatory Code of Conduct to ensure appropriate compliance with all national and international labour standards by the manufacturers and production workshops. A copy of this signed by each supplier can be viewed at the Mango offices.

We have set out below the subjects covered by the Code, based on ILO agreements and recommendations and the Mango group's own values and principles:

1. *Child labour*

   The manufacturers and workshops may not use nor support the use of child labour as defined in the ILO agreements.

2. *Forced and mandatory labour*

   The workshops and manufacturers may not use any form of forced or mandatory labour.

3. *Health and safety in the workplace*

   With respect to the general awareness in existence about the risks involved in their industry in general, as well as any risks specific to their industry, the workshops and manufacturers shall provide a safe and healthy working environment, and shall take all appropriate measures to prevent risks, accidents and injuries occurring during working activities or associated therewith, by restricting as far as is reasonably practical, the causes of risks inherent in said working environment

4. *Freedom of association and the right of collective bargaining*

   The workshops and manufacturers shall respect the rights of their employees to assemble, to organize or to bargain collectively and the employees shall suffer no kind of sanction in respect thereof.

5. *Discrimination*

   The workshops and manufacturers shall neither adopt nor support any form of discrimination based on the characteristics of race, nationality, religion, handicap, sex, sexual orientation, political affiliation or association in matters of recruiting, paying, training, promoting, dismissing or retiring their personnel.

6. *Disciplinary measures, harassment and abuse*

The workshops and manufacturers shall neither employ nor support the use of physical punishment, mental or physical pressure, nor of physical or psychological abuse or of any other kind of harassment.

7. *Working hours*

The workshops and manufacturers shall comply with the legislation in force and the rules governing their industry in the matter of work hours.

8. *Payment*

The workshops and manufacturers shall guarantee that the wages paid are strictly in keeping with all laws.

9. *Environment*

All activities in the workshops and manufacturers' premises shall be undertaken in such a way as to preserve the environment.

10. *Compliance with legislation in force*

The workshops and manufacturers shall at all times abide by the laws in force in the various environments applicable.

11. *Scope of application of the Code*

All the points set out above must of necessity be applied to all the manufacturers and workshops with which the Mango group works.

In order to achieve this objective, the manufacturers and workshops shall authorize the Mango group to carry out inspections, or to order them to be carried out by third parties, to monitor the application of this Code. They shall also allow the inspectors' access to all documentation and devices necessary to guarantee the viability of this process.

12. *Implementation and coming into force of the Code*

The Mango group shall agree to take positive measures to implement the Code and to incorporate it into all its operations and to make it an integral part of their overall philosophy and general policy.

13. *Acceptance and commitment on the part of the manufacturers and workshops*

All the manufacturers and workshops shall accept and make commitments to comply with all the points laid down in this Code by means of their signature and stamp on each page of the document in question. A signed copy shall always be available on Mango's premises.

14. *Subsequent adaptations and updates*

Any adaptation or update to which the Code of Conduct may be subject shall take the form of documents attached thereto, notwithstanding the previous point.

15. *Monitoring the application of the Code*

The Department of Corporate Social Responsibility, in concert with the departments involved in contracting and managing the manufacturers and workshops, shall pay regular follow-up visits, according to criteria that may be established at any time and in keeping with an annual programme.

In order to perform this monitoring procedure, the manufacturers (concerned with production characteristics) will remain informed at all times about the factories where they produce the garments or accessories so that the Mango organization, in keeping with the provisions covering this point, will ensure that this Code is followed. It will also be the duty of these organizations (manufacturers) to communicate to the various factories their obligations to observe and abide by this Code by signing it at the commencement of activities.

16. *Collaboration with non-governmental organizations and other bodies*

The Mango group will sign mutual collaboration agreements with NGOs to achieve positive consolidation and progress in these areas. With this in mind, inspection visits will be paid to the manufacturers and workshop operators' premises in the company of the representatives of these NGOs, with the objective of collaborating on those aspects in respect of which, as far as is possible and in keeping with the applicable legislation in each country, they can achieve a framework of mutual collaboration. These inspections could take place at the same time as supervision and monitoring visits. In addition, these inspections would also be designed to make transparent the provision of corporate responsibility policy information as pertains to the various manufacturers and production workshops.

17. *Remedial actions*

Any situation that would lead to any suspicion that the above points were being breached would call for immediate remedial action by the manufacturer or workshop. Should it be necessary to implement and monitor such remedial actions, this would be arranged with the manufacturers and workshops with a timetable worked out for their implementation. From this point of view, Mango would play a part in these actions by contributing technical support.

Should a serious social emergency situation arise (child labour, forced labour, etc.) or some other important occurrence affecting the manufacturers and workshops, and the required remedial measures are not immediately implemented, Mango will terminate its relationship with the manufacturer or workshop in question.

Before the initiation of any activities with the suppliers, an initial analysis and verification will be carried out to ensure that all of the points in the Code of Conduct are being observed in all of the work centres.

However, because of the characteristics of the production system, quality control teams (specialist technical personnel hired by Mango) are available in the same locations where manufacturing is done. These teams will inspect different factories and workshops on a daily basis and undertake inspections of the quality and number of garments produced plus any other aspect of their manufacture.

In addition, since they are in constant contact with the suppliers, at the same time that the teams monitor production, they continually check that no breaches of the Code of Conduct take place.

The CSR Audit Department also performs checks and audits to monitor supplier compliance with the Code. These audits, performed in company with labour union representatives when they occur, cover the following actions:

1. Interviewing the heads and/or owners of the factories and workshops with a view to securing all necessary information relating to the various labour, social and environmental aspects and also the procedures associated with them;

2. An exhaustive inspection of the factory installation, including filming and photographing them from top to bottom;

3. The selection of a sample of employees from the personnel lists of the supplier and/or production line management, to be interviewed on all aspects of the Code drawn up by Mango with particular reference to payroll matters (minimum wages, overtime payments, etc.).

The totality of the data obtained will be used to produce a Code of Conduct Compliance Report, plus a report detailing a series of recommendations to be applied to all of these aspects. If any remedial action is necessary, a timetable will be drawn up for that purpose.

The suppliers will also be monitored by the performance of an external audit that will begin with the same kind of interview as described above, but will also include an exhaustive review of the factory installations, with all units being photographed and recorded.

If labour unions are in existence, the procedure will take place in the presence of union representatives.

As a final step, the company will issue a certificate of compliance to the supplier, together with the report including the recommendations regarding the aspects analyzed.

At the present time, Mango handles quality control and external and in-house audits in all the countries where it produces its garments and accessories.

The in-house and external audits take place within the first three months of authorization by Mango to commence production, which always follows the initial check of CSR made by the Purchasing Department and Quality Control.

In all cases where one or more breaches of the Code are identified, a deadline is given for remedial action as laid down in the Code itself.

Should any incident among CSR agreement participants be identified by a local labour union, the incident will be analyzed and a solution decided upon in concert with the union in question and together with the organizations involved.

2. Environmental policy and management system

In 2008, an in-house environmental management system called the Mango Environmental Management System (SGMM) was put into effect at the installations and distribution centres in Spain. The SGMM includes all aspects included in the ISO 14001 certification and is more specific than the standard system imposed. It dictates the company's environmental policy in detail and a description of the management and monitoring of the system in its various areas of application, including among other things, areas such as training, communications or environmental best practice guidelines.

The nature of Mango's activities means that there are two different fields of environmental management, one in-house, the other external.

From the in-house point of view this activity basically takes place with regard to the Mango plant, product and shops; the external aspect fundamentally applies to the factories and the distribution and supply field, since all the production and logistics are in the hands of third parties. Mango regards the shops as part of their in-house management, whether they are their own or franchises, since the systems, materials and operating characteristics are the same.

During 2009, the first stage of a study of greenhouse gas emissions was conducted. This initial stage covers the period from the finished product to its sale at a shop, and as far as emissions are concerned, it is the area of greatest importance and impact. The second stage, which is planned for the third quarter of 2010, will examine the supply of goods and the manufacture of garments and accessories. It should be recalled that the Ecology and Development organization (ECODES) has examined this stage of the study, awarding Mango the $ZeroCO_2$ accreditation label as verification.

The textiles organization is also provided with a packaging and packing residue provision plan that has been passed by the authorities, and that covers the following:

- Minimizing the size of cases as far as technically possible to avoid breakages and crushing;
- The establishment of a minimum size for labelling to facilitate accurate reading;
- As far as possible, the reduction of individual packaging used for articles and accessories, both in dimensions and density. The aim is to prevent breakage and facilitate delivery by the distribution machines.
- The cases used are made from 100 per cent recycled material. For increased recovery, all seals are made from paper and no metal elements are used.

In recent years, considerable reductions in packaging have been made possible by the preparation of orders without packaging or warehousing, or cross-docking, as it is known. This covers some 20 per cent of production, practically the entire first season's shop deliveries.

As previously explained, this system consists of the suppliers' preparation and packing specific orders for garments and accessories in accordance with the instructions issued by Mango, that are expected to arrive at the shops with their original cases and packaging. This is a very modern logistics system since it cuts the use of all kinds of packaging almost by half, thereby consuming less energy and fewer resources, since merchandise is no longer sorted twice and warehousing costs are considerably reduced.

At the present moment this system applies only to the first deliveries to shops, since restocking takes place from the central warehouses, and includes folded garments, which represent 80 per cent of the collections.

3. Social action

Our chapter on Corporate Social Responsibility also highlights Mango's commitment to society in general by its active participation in various social projects, both directly and via specialist organizations. Sometimes it does this by funding specific projects in needy countries and sometimes by collaborating with non-economic projects such as donations of clothing or offering personnel support. In 2004 this collaboration policy was made official, and actions were mainly directed towards supporting basic education in developing countries.

Below we have listed some of the most significant projects in which Mango has been involved.

Vicente Ferrer Foundation

Mango helped this foundation build four communities (110 homes), eight of which were adapted for people with disabilities in the Gooty region (Anantapur). The Gooty region is located in the Indian state of Andhra Pradesh where this foundation is active. Mango has collaborated closely with them since 2004.

Mutual Missionary Support Service of the Catalan and Balearic Capuchins (SSIM)

The Mango group has taken part in the second stage of building an integrated development centre for homeless boys and girls at risk of social exclusion in the town of Florencia, Department of Caquetá, (Colombia).

Active Africa

Support for this organization takes the form of funding for the rehabilitation of the primary school in Mvera, Malawi. Academically, this primary school was traditionally seen as one of the best in the region. Active Africa is a Catalan NGO involved in humanitarian development projects in Africa.

Médecins sans Frontières [Doctors without Borders]

Mango was involved in a pediatric and reproductive campaign in Karamoja (Uganda), the aim of which was to reduce mortality rates among mothers and children by upgrading existing structures and setting up a network of eight mobile clinics. Mango financed the medical team, the laboratory and the rehabilitation of the existing clinics.

The Integra Foundation

Mango is involved with its integration programs by hiring individuals who are members of groups at risk of social exclusion, thus promoting social inclusion and integration.

The Ágata [Agate] *Association*

Mango shared in funding the lease of their premises in Barcelona. The purpose of this centre is to act as a meeting point for breast cancer patients where they can receive psychological support and information, and make contact with other women who either suffer from this disease or who have beaten it.

The ACAB Association

> The purpose of this association is to combat anorexia and bulimia. Mango has taken part in the *Reemprender el camino* [Getting back on track] project by financing three workshops for people who have completed the treatment and are now outpatients. The aim of Mango's involvement is to support and facilitate the integration of these eating disorder sufferers back into their academic, social and employment environments, provide support systems and prevent relapses.

Ravaltex, the social inclusion company

> Mango has worked with this organization by passing them the work of making alterations to garments required by customers of their shops in Barcelona. This organization also produces samples for the public relations department.

4. Quality management systems associated with the CSR

Since 2001, a quality control system has been in place that complies with International Standard ISO 9001:2000, which covers all the departments that have direct contact with the product at any stage in its production.

This system is based on areas that are management strengths and that are regarded as crucial for the future development of the system. Attention should be drawn to the following among them:

- Quality control teams that monitor and support the suppliers, both from a head office base and directly within the factories. This direct monitoring is undertaken by teams that reside in the main production zones and work in the remote technical offices;

- Permanent certification and inspection of supplier factories, in line with the specifications laid down by the quality control system, Quality Mango System (QMS), and undertaken directly by the teams in question;

- Updating, giving instructions and constantly monitoring the suppliers regarding the physical characteristics (composition, shrinkage, etc.) of the garments and the components of the garments and accessories;

- Permanent updating and optimization of the process maps, with a view to continual improvement.

An interactive and two-way ICT application has been implemented between the suppliers and the design, purchasing and quality teams that makes it possible to manage all the information relating to the general processes, specific features of the season and all of the aspects arising from each of the models dispatched (pricing, patterns, technical follow-up, comments, times, etc.). This system, bolstered by the factors detailed in the section about product characteristics, sets down high quality standards for the suppliers and their factories (capacity, experience, globalization, organization, etc.) that are reflected in all aspects as well as in the CSR, which has constant support from the abovementioned quality control teams.

Manufacturers' raw materials

All the suppliers of the finished products receive written instructions from Mango regarding the standards for the use of products and substances in the manufacturing process, applicable also to the raw materials that they themselves buy.

Once the production process has started, these substances are monitored by exhaustive analysis that is then applied to all of the articles produced.

This verification procedure is carried out by selecting specific garments and/or accessories from each sample group, according to the statistical criteria established and then sending them to a laboratory for full analysis. The laboratory issues a certificate for all the articles.

The selection of samples for analysis is always done with finished garments and accessories, since changes to fabrics and their components and materials during handling by the supplier may occur during the design process and first production tests.

In the previously mentioned supplier instructions, both those substances which are regulated as well as those that may not be regulated by laws in various countries are pointed out. These latter substancesare also monitored and checked in compliance with specific statistical criteria.

Raw materials in the production workshops

Unlike the manufacturers' system, on each occasion when raw materials are acquired by the workshops, Oeko-Tex certification is sought for all the textiles. This certification is issued by laboratories authorized in each country by the Swiss organization Oeko-Tex. Once this certification is obtained, Mango sends the raw materials to the suppliers for production.

This certification requires much more stringent controls than that laid down by the laws of various countries, both because a greater number of substances identified by this organization are checked and because lower tolerance limits than those laid down by various laws for some substances are applied.

There are operational reasons for applying different management schemes according to the manufacturing systems described above.

10

Sharing Company Values

E nric Casi says that the people who work at Mango share the company's values because it is important for the people who work there to make it feel like a family – so that it really *is* a company.

This is a progressive company and its growth is based on the people who form part of the organization. From this point of view, Mango gives priority to in-house promotion, for example, (notwithstanding the possibility of talented candidates being taken on from outside the company) to fill vacancies in any of its departments. In this way it takes care of its staff's personal and professional satisfaction and the staff in turn, feel motivated to perform their daily activities. In actual fact, practically all of the managers and team heads in the organization attained these positions of responsibility thanks to in-house promotion. In 2009, some 14.29 per cent of head office staff were promoted. If we extend the number to include shop staff, internal promotion covers a very respectable 10.15 per cent.

This and other factors, such as its international projection, Code of Ethics and innovations have turned Mango into one of the most sought-after employers.

The employees maintain continual dialogue with shareholders and staff, including managers, through meetings entitled "If I were president." These meeting are organized in several steps. In the first step, the members of each department take a vote to choose a representative who cannot be either a team leader or the head of the department. This person calls all the members of the department to a meeting where all the ideas, suggestions, changes or improvements to be subsequently tabled at the meeting are aired.

These representatives then meet with the management, shareholders and directors to communicate the various proposals.

The conclusions, changes and improvements agreed to are published and communicated to all the employees in the company's in-house newsletters. The effectiveness of this initiative is reflected in the fact that 95 per cent of the proposals discussed at these meetings end up as actual changes (adaptation of working hours, leave arrangements, improvements and extensions of services, improvements in the safety or ergonomics and comfort of work positions, and so on).

With a view to encouraging participation in this dialogue, in April 2007 a survey was conducted by an external company in which 2,380 staff members (69 per cent of the workforce) took part. The result of this study served as a sound foundation for improvements that contributed to management's success.

Employees are provided with their own portal on the company intranet just for their use where detailed and up-to-date information can be found regarding human resources administration, selection and training. This portal is also used to manage personal data or leave schedules, check salaries, investigate and apply for training courses, find information about vacancies, etc.

Encouraging teamwork is another important point in Mango's staff policy. With this in mind, Mango launched two initiatives: a suggestion box and brainstorming sessions, wherein all employees may contribute ideas and proposals designed to help the organization operate more efficiently.

Mango's CSR policy is also linked to promotion and, in general, to making the employees' lives easier, for example, by reconciling family and work. In this respect, after the birth of a child and for one year, the company facilitates work time changes for the parents without them needing to apply for a shorter working day. Maternal leave allowances are also in place so that female employees can continue to receive 100 per cent of their salaries. While on maternity leave the company also pays all extra payments corresponding to employees during this time. In the case of full-time employees, once back at work, the mother can also choose between a one-hour reduction per working day for nursing, or she can accumulate these hours and take additional time off, since these hours come to 19 working days additional leave.

Also important in reconciling home and work, flexitime is facilitated to meet employees' personal needs, including temporary contract suspension on the same grounds, with the employees continuing to retain their jobs in these cases. The organization also allows ample time for doctor's visits.

Working hours are established with the consensus of the employees (office staff, for example, are allowed to extend their days by half an hour in order to finish at midday on Friday). This means that employees can enjoy a shorter day on the eve of the main festivals. In departments or sections where this is operationally possible, this option is implemented throughout the year.

The company also provides financial bonuses for employees who marry, establish *de facto* relationships or have a child. The organization head office is equipped with a number of dining rooms available for employees who bring packed lunches and those employees who choose to eat in the company's cafeterias pay only 30 per cent of the cost. On a daily basis, some 600 meals are served and if employees wish, they may order these meals 'to go' and take them home with them.

The contractual model reveals that 94.05 per cent of the staff are permanent, and 5.95 per cent temporary. In the case of the shops, 66.11 per cent are permanent and 32.89 per cent temporary. Full-time employees in Spain represent 56.13 per cent of the workforce, and part-time staff, 43.87 per cent. In the case of their foreign subsidiaries, these percentages stand at 85.69 per cent and 14.31 per cent respectively.

If we glance at the equal opportunity situation, we notice three relevant factors. Some 40.52 per cent of managerial positions are held by women. Worldwide, women are in the majority, both as full-time staff (60.56 per cent) and particularly as far as the shops are concerned. The average age of employees is 31.

And finally, the geographical breakdown by age group reveals that in Spain, 55.5 per cent of employees are aged between 26 and 35, while abroad some 53.25 per cent are aged between 16 and 25.

One effect of the business becoming global is that the company's employees represent a huge range of cultures. In the head office, employees represent a number of different nationalities, as in the shops and offices in various countries. Professionals from China, Bulgaria, the USA, France, Guinea, Israel, Ireland, Japan, Italy, Morocco, Mexico, the Dominican Republic, Sweden, Venezuela and other nations work for the company, which may add up to as many as 30 different nationalities being represented.

On the labour relations front, the company's outstanding Work Hazard Prevention manual was developed by the company's technical staff and covers procedures designed and implemented to tackle this area in the company. These procedures are continually revised and changed to accommodate new requirements that may arise in order to ensure that risk prevention is as good as it can be.

Training in work hazard prevention for the shop staff is carried out via the company's intranet. Checks are carried out in order to guarantee that training has been completed and relevant certificates applied for.

Prevention monitoring affects data display screen users, as well as staff exposed to possible untenable noise, lighting or even temperatures, among others factors.

The Mango group defends its commitment to all labour relationships to ensure that they exist within a framework of fairness that defends the basic rights and principles of the individual. Thus one of Mango's commitments is to never employ anyone who has not yet reached the legal age to work and to use no forms of forced or mandatory labour.

The company also ensures that its employees carry out their work in a safe and healthy environment and does not tolerate discrimination of any kind based on race, nationality, religion, disability, sex, sexual orientation, political association or affiliation.

On the remuneration front, the company is also committed to ensuring that salaries match the duties performed and the dedication required in terms of hours worked. This always functions within the framework laid down by the laws of each country.

Mango's commitment to its employees is also in line with its policy whereby remuneration should match each situation. In the case of full-time employees, (consisting of approximately 1,700 people), salaries are assessed, balanced and matched to the duties and professional development of each employee twice a year. As regards the shop sales staff, the system is based on fixed income plus bonuses based on shop turnover.

Mango is proud of the fact that its salaries are above average for the sector. In real terms, the ratio between the average starting salary fixed by the Catalan company and the minimum wage is some 50.53 per cent higher for Spain. And as time passes, salaries rise with incentives and promotions that substantially increase this difference.

All employees, full-time and part-time, have the same rights and social benefits. The company is also very assiduous when it comes to developing policies which prevent income discrimination between men and women.

Mango has implemented a policy of ongoing training and there is a special department that handles both its technical needs (languages, office automation, etc.) and human requirements (personal growth, values, team management, etc.). Most of this training takes place in classrooms at the head office.

Working with various department heads, this team handles and promotes applications for professional courses, university qualifications, etc. In 2009, training courses reached a total of 71,063 hours and benefited 7,051 people.

The Catalan company sees training as essential for maintaining a positive work climate, and is aware of the problems and weaknesses that arise without ongoing training.

Part of the attention paid to the countless small details which favour a good work climate is informality in business dealings, regardless of the individual's professional role. Andic and Casi have worked to maintain this basic feel of a small and modest company, regardless of the size it has now reached. They are the first to implement this closeness, which is much appreciated by their staff, irregardless of rank distinctions or responsibilities.

The company benefits from this 'close-up and personal' style, because it means that it is easier to share and solve problems. At the same time, good ideas can be shared, ideas that can come from any part of the organization, and that support the sense experienced by everyone that they can participate in and promote creativity.

It isn't just football that makes its supporters want to wear the team strip. A good company can also communicate passion, or at least rouse corporate appeal and admiration. All of this is achieved on the basis of everything the brand represents, both from its public and in-house projections. The aim is to develop loyalty in the hearts of the talented, so that they will stay. From this point of view, Mango has achieved both objectives, by becoming a brand with values that has an international presence, thanks to continual improvements in management policies.

In concrete terms, this approach, based on familiarity and the desire to motivate its employees, is perfectly defined by coach and coordinator of the Master's Degree in Personal Development and Leadership at Barcelona University, Irene Orce, when she says, "Mango is a company which offers opportunities for high quality personal and professional development. It is outstanding as a company in constant evolution, committed to innovation and overcoming the endless challenges presented by the market, and with the power to do so. It operates with transparent and fluent communications, based on continual dialogue between staff and management. It is also based on the creation of sustainable value and has accepted the duty of being a socially responsible company, generating quality jobs with flexible working conditions. This is why it defends reconciliation and flexibility as guidelines for development, binding good wages to high health and safety standards in the workplace."

11 | Mango on the Internet

M ango is characterized as a very dynamic company, partly because its structure is extremely open to change and prepared to accept new challenges. Its growth on various platforms it has developed for using the internet, and its use of the internet for communications, are evidence of this dynamism and capacity to adapt to new realities. Its internet strategy is contained within that general concept that Andic defined when he said that it was the concept which must remain unchanged, not the formulae for achieving those objectives.

Adaptation to this new digital world offers great advantages to those companies able to adapt to trends and make them their own. Conversely, Mango operates in opposition to those companies that insist on remaining at the fringe of the phenomenon, particularly when it is already a fact that most consumers, including the target public of many businesses, are connected to the internet.

From very early on, Mango has been able to take great advantage of the internet and this has helped it get ahead of many of its competitors. It even jumped ahead of some of the fashion greats, such as Ralph Lauren, which was very slow to launch its own website (in the case of the US designer, this was not until 2000). The Catalan group was able to align its strategy with both the medium and its customers' needs, setting itself apart from many other important companies in the sector. Convinced that an internet presence was essential, the company has never ceased strengthening its investment in innovative actions wherever its public is to be found.

As quoted in the book *Zara and her Sisters,* by Enrique Badía (Palgrave Macmillan), MangoShop was a pioneer in Spanish textiles when it developed a sales channel on the internet. This channel not only served as a medium to communicate marketing actions since 1996, it has also been a sales channel of ever-increasing importance.

The business sector has probably not understood the use of the internet very well. This timidity when it comes to using new technologies has a direct relationship with the fact that the sales volume achieved by the fashion industry by this means is still modest. However, there are many positive factors that support a more direct strategy. In its favour, for example, is the fact that Mango targets a young, urban and savvy public, which effectively describes most internet users. In Mango's case, many of its consumers are women with this particular social and professional profile who use of the internet for shopping because of their long working hours and personal activities that leave little time for shopping.

The profile of the woman who buys her clothes at Mango is the same as that of the woman who shops on the internet. The online shop represents one more shop for this purchaser and offers the added advantage of being open 24 hours a day throughout the year, so she can shop without leaving home, and receive her order in just a few days (between two and five) without having to pay delivery costs. In addition, exchanges and returns are streamlined so that customers can do this at any of the group's shops. In other words, Mango's relationship with its customers is unrestricted.

Despite these kinds of exposure, Mango's products are not easy to sell on the internet. Sometimes offering the latest trend involves certain disadvantages with this medium. To avoid them, garments on offer have been previously selected with a careful eye to the consumer's needs (sizes are specified, the line, fabric and composition and washing instructions are specified) and photographs have a very neutral presentation so that the customer can get a genuine idea of what the product is and not experience any unpleasant surprises when the goods are delivered.

Thanks to the high level of market penetration, customers who buy at Mangoshop usually know the brand very well. This is a great help, since the purchaser is familiar with the standards of quality and cut. It would be much more difficult to sell their fashions if their brand were not so well known.

Exemplary development: from the static website to the dynamic blog.

1996 Birth of the mango.com website

2000 MangoShop.com Europa

2006 MangoShop USA and Canada; Opening of MangoOutlet.com

2007 Birth of weblet QueMePongoByMango.com

2008 Birth of website hominiemerito.com

2009 Launch of the official MANGO page and official mangoshop page on Facebook

2010 Appearance of keepthebeat.mango.com blog and app for the iPhone

2010 MangoShop Turkey, China, Korea and Japan

1. 1996: The launch of the Mango.com website

The Mango.com site was launched in 1996 with the main objective of offering corporate information and displaying products to the business world with a view to capturing new franchisees. Apart from the information about the company, the shops and an explanation of how to open a Mango franchise, 20 images were selected from that season's catalogue in order to to show off a part of the collection.

Later on, the company discovered the huge communication potential of this platform and for the following season published the entire catalogue online.

Their website is also a potent channel for recruitment since as of the close of 2009, 45 per cent of the total of job applications received came from there.

2. 2000: The development of a new sales channel

Four years later, in 2000, the company launched sales via the internet with MangoShop. This presence is both an added value for the company and a point of sale. In any case this is not a question of image, but of service, since it is seen as a good way to approach customers who find it difficult to get to the physical shops, for whatever reason.

In recent years it has become established as a channel and has experienced double-digit growth every year. Its percentage turnover compared with total sales has also grown in recent years, although it remains relatively small.

Figure 11.1 Total Turnover for Online Sales in Spain.

	€ Total t/o	€ Online t/o	Increase	Wt.
2005	888.260	2.187	—	0,2%
2006	990.960	3.800	74%	0,4%
2007	1.104.877	5.930	56%	0,5%
2008	1.140.943	8.000	35%	0,7%
2009	1.145.156	11.700	46%	1,0%

(Source: MANGO)

Gradually this sales channel extended internationally, and once the rest of Europe was covered, it became available in the United States and Canada (2006) and Japan, Korea, Turkey and China (2010). Indeed, this extensive geographical spread is one of the keys to the success of this platform according to the company.

At the same time, in 2006 the company opened MangoOutlet.com, a website which makes garments from previous seasons available to the public at reduced prices.

Mango's major competitors have adopted very different strategies regarding internet sales. On the one hand H&M, also a pioneer, launched its online presence in 1998. The Swedish company selectively established its online companies in relation to online access and use in different countries. At the present time it operates in Sweden (since 1998), Denmark and Finland (1999), Norway (2001), the Netherlands (2006) and Germany and Austria (2007).

The other significant case would be Zara, which has remained on the margin and delayed its internet development. Inditex say that fast-changing fashions and the constant renewal of its items have rendered online management very difficult. The first brand in the group that got involved with internet sales was Zara Home (since 2007). The autumn-winter collection for 2010 was the occasion of the launch of Zara, the Inditex flagship. At the moment, you can only buy their products in Spain, Portugal, France, the UK, Germany and Italy, but the rest of the countries where the company has a physical presence will be progressively included. Inditex has no plans to develop an online presence for the rest of its brands in the near future.

3. 2007: *What Should I Wear by Mango* and the 2.0 communities

Between autumn and winter 2007 Mango introduced the website *What Should I Wear by Mango,* and this greatly affected its internet strategy by stimulating interaction with consumers through dialogue and exchanges of experiences. The aim of the new website was to respond to all the questions and comments received from customers about the collections, via direct communication. This new channel granted customers the capability of consulting with the company on matters of style and receiving advice on everyday fashion matters. The consumers could also view information about the group's new products or business lines. By using this dynamic environment,

Mango has been adapting to fashion trends and has updated its content on a weekly basis.

Following Mango's usual promotion formula, the website uses professionals who are deeply committed to the fashion world, such as models, bloggers or style gurus with international reputations. The name and brand image is often buttressed by the presence of famous fashion personalities such as Dakota Johnson, Eugenia Silva, Goya Toledo, Hugo Sauzay, Ariadne Artiles, Nuno Lopes, Dree Hemingway and Laura Ponte, among others. As with the company's other website launches, to open this minisite they commissioned an advertising campaign that appeared on all the main television networks.

Mango's effort to upgrade their interactivity with users has resulted in improvements to various versions of the website, such as connecting comments with profiles on the social network Facebook.

Given the global nature of the company, the website is available in several languages.

The creation of this platform on the internet marked the company's first step towards more direct communication with customers and helped to establish a more consistent relationship with these women. Their opinions are courted on notice boards and blogs, thereby establishing and facilitating broad interactivity. Since it was launched, *What Should I Wear by Mango* has been a great success, reflected in the site's high number of visitors who, thanks to their opinions, have helped streamline the content and form of the website, season after season.

4. 2010: Internet 2.0

In March 2010 Mango launched their *Keep the beat* blog with the aim of securing brand loyalty from web surfers via more direct communication and informal language. The content includes information about trends and innovations in fashion and lifestyle, the arrival of collections to the points of sale, announcements about collaboration initiatives with other brands and designers, etc. Overall, the aim is to keep the faithful informed from the heart of Mango so that they always have the latest information and their loyalty to the brand is secured.

As we read in the chapter on celebrities and new opinion leaders, and as Montse Escobar, expert in influence-related communications at the advertising agency Grey articulates, "The blog phenomenon was created at the opening of the 21st century by a handful of American authors who found themselves fielding millions of visits to their pages. The next thing they knew they were being invited to parties and events. The phenomenon has arrived in Spain with a vengeance, and even though our bloggers don't achieve the same figures, their importance is no less relevant." Escobar also points out that "the numbers of visits to Spanish blogs are always lower, and few visits are spontaneous since most of them come from links."

This phenomenon is reflected in the business strategies of brands great and small and they usually set up their own blogs, as Mango has done. Associated with this phenomenon and the rise of social networks is the appearance of the community manager, who manages the company's internet image. When no specialist team exists, the community manager can also boost the company's internet profiles or pages and supply content to the blogs, all with a focus that is much more personal than commercial.

In addition to this, Mango has also invested a lot of effort on new platforms such as social networks (it has been on Facebook since 2009) or mobile platforms via the launch of an iPhone app (2010) that keeps users up to date with brand innovations and promotions, and locations of stores and the like. These are available in Spanish, English, French and German and can be used for purchasing products on the internet as well as for 'trying them on' by using the virtual interactive model, which uses the customer's own photograph.

By means of these technologies Mango has succeeded in building a much stronger relationship with its customers and being where they are, plus allowing them to easily access the company by any of the means discussed. Moreover, the input from users has been crucial to upgrading the company's internet strategy and ensuring that it does what it should.

5. In-house internet management

These new channels are structured by two teams in-house: the e-business team (who handle the corporate website and virtual shops), plus a second team who form a part of Marketing and Advertising, and who specialize in these new media. The e-business department manages all the internet platforms, the company's intranet and extranet as well as electronic business and they perform these duties in collaboration with the Customer Service, Logistics and Transportation, Legal and Administration and Exports departments.

The whole scenario is brought together via communications activities, work that is now partly outsourced to agencies that specialize in design and internet business development. Even so, in all of these cases, the technology is still owned by the company and has been customized for their purposes.

6. Sales on other platforms

Eager to grow its internet sales channel, Mango decided to develop its presence on the most powerful internet sales channels in the country. Hence it can be found on asos.com, the main internet sales channel in the UK, and on privalia.com, in Spain. It has also signed agreements with the main Chinese and American channels.

Mango's CEO explains the steps the company has taken on the internet: "This is an indispensable strategy if you want to grow on this channel. Internet sale channels owned by the businesses themselves might account for between 1 per cent and 2 per cent of total sales turnover, but other alternatives can make up the greater part of the growth since their strategy is much more focused on this kind of selling." Casi has remarked, "thanks to these specialist channels, online channels may make up between 6 per cent and 8 per cent of turnover in the next two years."

As Damián Sánchez is wont to comment, the online channel is not only important as far as image is concerned; it also provides very direct information about the consumer. There have been times when the company has had to ask blog readers which celebrities they would choose for upcoming campaigns, and via the internet, the company can obtain in-depth knowledge of each customer's personal preferences, thanks to a record of their purchases, so that similar products can be offered at another time.

This strategy, like the others that are media focused, is defined by the company itself as a holistic (360 degrees) and innovative strategy that succeeds in placing the brand in first position on the preference lists of its target public; it also clearly projects the values and essence of the Mango brand. This strategy increases the company's database records regarding customers whose loyalty it will later attempt to secure. And, of course, it also performs a traditional commercial function in that it strives to increase sales. As far as internet sales are concerned, traditional obstacles such as the following have been overcome: the lack of security and trust on the part of the user, not being able to try the garments on and the absence of key senses such as touch and smell, thanks to careful and close interaction with the individual user through personalized recommendations of advisors, celebrities or other users.

In light of all of these factors, we can say that not only has Mango managed to adapt to the new era; it has also managed to establish trends and take the leading position among its competitors. It has managed to successfully adapt the marketing formula of each channel (physical or interactive) without losing sight of its customers' preferences. The figures prove this, and it merits noting that on all its internet channels it has managed to record double-digit growth in website traffic:

Figure 11.2 Individual visits to the company's various websites.

	2008	2009	Growth
www.mango.com	13.861.657	16.430.996	18,5%
www.mangoshop.com	9.378.623	15.898.970	69,5%
www.mangooutlet.com	2.220.375	3.236.203	45,8%
www.quemepongobymango.com	992.471	1.290.200	30,0%
www.mangofashionawards.com	207.949	238.123	14,5%

(Source: Mango)

12

Men's Fashions and the HE Line

Throughout the history of design, men's fashions have occupied a secondary position since both socially and artistically it was assumed that garments aimed at men would lack the charm and magic associated with women's fashions. Psychoanalysts such as J.C. Flügel state that men have not competed with women in fashion since the first half of the last century. Even so, we can all visualize the elegant gentleman's suits of the beginning of the twentieth century, the beauty in the cut and drape and their smart accessories. In its various reincarnations, the men's suit enjoyed lasting success, and has even had a considerable effect on women's fashions.

But in any case, men's fashions have clearly developed differently from women's. This development followed an exponential trajectory, and in recent years has taken centre stage because of new concepts of masculinity. Men's fashion is becoming important again on the catwalks. And while for some time now men have become increasingly interested in fashion matters, little by little a new kind of masculinity has made its appearance with the birth of a new stereotype for men known as the 'metrosexual,' nowadays accepted by the majority along with many other changes. Now the masculine sector can also include a concern for fashion and an interest in trends. These changes toward a new definition of the relationship between the sexes infer a change in mentality and a step closer to equality, as well.

Emerging from the shadows of a succession of historically important individuals from the last century, this paradigm change has penetrated society in a number of ways.

Despite its delayed development, the influence of men's fashion on women's fashion is certainly beyond doubt (much more so than vice-versa). Clear evidence of this is the adaptation by women of traditionally male garments such as suits, trousers or shirts, items which now form part of a woman's fashion palette on their own account.

Men's fashion and its importance in the industry today cannot be ignored. Communications media, perfumes and men's collections inspired by and initially following lines dictated by women's fashion, corroborate this fact that is also strengthened by sociological factors such as new forms of defining masculinity and more sexual freedom.

In its early years, Mango offered both men's and women's fashions, but in 1988 the pressure to expand the company led Isak Andic and his team to stake everything on women as their target public.

Why did they focus on women? Although in the 1980s, men's fashions were established and greatly impacted the most famous designers, Andic and his team chose to focus on women's clothing because of the simplicity of design of the garments which did not require the complex design and production work involved in making men's jackets and overcoats. Twenty years on, Mango is rethinking its focus, seeing men as valued consumers once again and therefore launching its own collection for the new male.

1. Development of men's fashions in the 20th century: From the static suit to the new masculinity

For women, the *roaring* 1920s marked an unprecedented step forward regarding freedom of expression. This was immediately reflected in fashion and aesthetics. Skirt hemlines rose and daring hairstyles appeared, along with shameless makeup and night life in jazz clubs where women could drink alcohol and smoke cigarettes. Designers such as Gabrielle 'Coco' Chanel established milestones in women's fashions during this period, breaking with classical canons that were baroque and over-elaborate, introducing new sober, elegant lines that were swiftly established among Parisians.

And yet, even though men's fashions certainly existed, this revolution passed them by. Between the 1920s and the end of World War II, men's fashion designs were characterized by the monotony and rigidity associated with the suit or the dinner jacket, with accessories distinguishing the individual man more than anything else: the walking stick, hat, gloves, watch and waistcoat, and of course, the handkerchief in the top jacket pocket.

After 1945, and until well into the 1950s, this fashion increasingly lost its dominance and yielded to more practical styles. Because they were all but useless, hats disappeared, and suits gave way to narrow, pressed, boot-cut trousers. Lapels and shirt collars also shrank and ties shrivelled to a normal width of barely three centimetres.

Elvis became an icon and James Dean who became a myth thanks to his early death in car accident in 1955, became fashion icons and stamped their images on the times where white t-shirts, jeans and boots predominated.

The end of the 1960s marked a 'before and after' moment in fashion that was now directly influenced by the most important social, cultural and economic events of the time:

- For the first time ever, fashion was born in the street, and alongside Paris, London became a world capital of fashion thanks to the trends generated by the *mod* movement and the influence of the Beatles and the Rolling Stones. This was the first time that music had an effect on the world of fashion and design, but it was certainly not the last. The garments that filled the display windows of Carnaby Street and King's Road boutiques became the paradigm that reflected the spirit of the style of 'swinging London'.

- The generation born after the war had concerns that were different from those of their parents and they built a new market around them. Fashion turned into a powerful tool for channeling the spirit of nonconformity and rebellion against the establishment. The hippie movement was born, which declared itself anti-fashion but helped to create a new and different style, one that lives on. Flared trousers appeared, checked and striped shirts and brightly coloured clothing, all as if to reflect the desire for freedom and rebellion against convention.

- Scientific advances (accompanied by the symbolic and actual climax of putting a man on the moon in 1969) were seen in fashion, especially in Europe. Innovations in fabrics (including metals, plastics and man-made fibres) and colours (neon or metallic) made their appearance. Art, too, had a direct influence on fashion, as shown in the designs of Paco Rabanne and Pierre Cardin.

The 1970s consolidated the trends born the previous decade, and elephant bells and platform shoes (for both sexes) were the stars. Disco music and dance floors were crucial to the trends that dominated men's style of the period: open-necked shirts, gold chains and light-coloured suits with big pointed shirt collars reflected the disco style that we saw in cinema with films such as *Saturday Night Fever*, starring the big name of the moment, John Travolta.

Once again, music left its mark on fashion in the 1970s, this time thanks to David Bowie, who together with others gave us glam rock style in his clothing, hairstyle and makeup. At the end of the decade we witnessed the punk movement, led by the Sex Pistols, that highlighted a trend still active today, characterized by an anti-system style and attitude that was and still is a great source of inspiration for today's designers. Men seek to share the limelight with women in the field of fashion and there is a rise in the number of designers presenting collections for men. This period has seen the rise of talents such as Paul Smith, who opened his first, humble shop in Nottingham, and whose distinguished detailing have put him among the top brands in men's fashions.

By the 1980s great designers such as Calvin Klein, Ralph Lauren, Giorgio Armani and Jean Paul Gaultier were beginning to launch men's collections. And alongside New York, Paris and Milan, the new decade saw Tokyo become a fashion capital with benchmark designers such as Yohji Yamamoto and Rei Kawakubo.

At the same time, the punk aesthetic and anti-fashion current was on the rise. Television series' such as *Miami Vice* (starring Don Johnson and Phillip Michael Thomas) and artists such as Michael Jackson and Prince exerted their own styles and these trends became fashion. The hip-hop movement created fashion from torn jeans, suits and the tracksuit.

Thenin the 1990s from Seattle, on the west coast of the USA, emerged a style of music espousing lack of hope for the future and attacking the pressures of the early1990s economic crisis, political instability and the 1993 war in the Middle East. Grunge (as the movement was dubbed) featuring long hair, striped shirts and jeans, and appeared with its own icon (Kurt Cobain and his band Nirvana). They communicated this despair both through their music and their appearance.

Concurrently, Tom Ford dominated as the star designer with his successful collections for both men and women for the Italian brand Gucci.

Although the emotional coldness associated with the image of the traditional man still persists, as the 21st century opens it brings the collapse of men's superiority over women in some parts of the world, and this has shattered traditional patterns for relationships between men and women.

Seen through the prism of the most traditional stereotypes, we would define the man of five decades ago as a worker, strongly disciplined and not particularly involved with the family. Thanks to greater sexual equality achieved in recent years, men are less likely to feel obligated to act brave, tough, hard and unfeeling, and can now allow themselves to feel and develop in ways that were probably taboo in the past and that they had to conceal, to avoid the shame of revealing their feelings in public.

The new masculinity has given rise to the metrosexual, and fashion is increasingly addressed towards men. The new male profile as a purchaser is an urban male who possesses a special taste for aesthetics, as reflected by his impeccable appearance. This new man is a great consumer of cosmetics and an avid reader of design magazines. He appreciates and compulsively seeks fashionable clothing, and attaches great value to brands.

In other words, the rise of this new masculinity and the appearance of new male consumer profiles are having a positive effect on the growth of the men's market for fashion companies. Mango has taken advantage of this and has accepted a new challenge: to establish itself as the leading company in the men's sector.

2. Homini Emerito and men's fashion according to Mango

In 2008, as part of this trend towards the new masculinity described above, Mango decided to re-start its men's collection with the brand name HE (Homini Emerito). This new line was pursued with a view to consolidating and increasing business figures. To achieve this, it was important to be aware that "men have changed and can now renew their wardrobe every season just because they like to follow the latest fashion trends," as Enric Casi put it.

The men's collection has been slowly growing at a steady rate (since competition is so fierce), but even after two years, this segment only represents a mere 1 per cent to 2 per cent of the company's total turnover.

The figure is not particularly symbolic compared with the women's sector, but the growth achieved in its second year (over 50 per cent) gives reasons to be optimistic for the future and some certainty that positive growth is sustainable. In this short period of time it has become clear that the brand that includes future sales volume and numbers of shops worldwide that equal those for the women's collection has great potential.

Management has recognized the fact that HE is still in its growth stage and this means that they are continually adjusting the profile of the *Mango man* as a step towards men identifying themselves with the brand, and subsequently becoming loyal to it. The men's line is associated with a man who is very committed to trends. Damián Sánchez says: "The profile of the HE buyer is that of someone who derives pleasure from being different, a rebel type who doesn't like rigid frameworks and who acts with a certain degree of independence. HE is a product which each man can adapt to his own appearance, from very formal to very sporty."

At this early stage, the men's fashion line has begun with the concept of the limited edition, with a view towards offering characteristics of exclusivity to customers in order to maintain a sustainable growth model, depending on demand and in-house adjustments in the way of creativity and design.

At this time, and bearing in mind that this is a strategic milestone, the HE collection is on display at 135 of the 1,400 shops, 9 per cent of Mango's shops. Good reception has been noted in markets as competitive as Italy, France, Germany and the UK, and also Andorra, Austria, Canada, Colombia, South Korea, the USA, Egypt, the United Arab Emirates, Spain, Israel, Peru, Portugal, the Czech Republic, Russia, Singapore, Syria, Switzerland and Turkey. The company is planning to open new men's shops in 2010 in Germany, the Netherlands and New Caledonia.

At this embryonic stage in the process that Enric Casi regards as a learning curve, merchandise is gradually being placed in women's points of sale, determined by space, customer numbers, optimum positioning and turnover volume. Barcelona stands as a special case and test bench, since there, the HE line occupies a greater display space than in Mango's other shops in Spain and also abroad.

According to Casi, the fact that at the present the collection is beside the women's line "is not a problem, since it produces positive synergies between both lines, such as offering products to young men accompanying their girlfriends buying clothes at Mango." Nevertheless, the objective is to keep growing with this line and eventually have both store and brand separate from the women's area.

Mango is planning four collections per year with two different lines following the design and production policy of the women's collection, at a lower level of production. One line will be casual, informal and more notable, and the other will be sober and classical. A line of accessories consisting of watches, handkerchiefs, bags and belts, among other things, is also being produced. As with the women's collection, HE garments are available online (Mango Shop) and also at the Mango Outlets. The line also has its own loyalty card.

The name is a statement of intent, since Homini Emerito implies a 'man who enjoys his rewards in keeping with his merits'. Such a man cannot wear just any old clothes, so the HE designs occupy more exclusive and less mass-market parameters than those of other fashion chains.

The ambience in the HE spaces is very different from that of the other Mango shops. They exude warmth, thanks to furnishings finished in black and gold, and a décor which includes antiques and leather chesterfields. Other details that lend character to this space are bevelled crystal, aged parquet flooring and carpeted walls displaying a unicorn, the logo of the collection. The fact that this line is smaller than other collections means it can be strategically located, with more space between items, with the HE décor assuming greater importance.

It is critical to bear in mind the fact that this shopping experience allows the brand to distinguish itself from some of its competitors, such as Zara or H&M, where visual appearance is not of primary importance in point of sale strategies. The images and music chosen, the amount of floorspace, the assistants and promotional elements such as the *Homini Emerito Newspaper* help the potential purchaser enjoy the transaction in a refined and relaxed atmosphere. HE is positioning itself among brands such as Abercrombie & Fitch, that are more concerned with the purchase experience than the product itself.

To promote this line, Mango has opted to collaborate with outstanding figures from the fashion worldsuch as models Jon Kortajarena and Vladimir Roitfeld (son of Carine Roitfeld, fashion world opinion leader and director of *Vogue France*), whose images help create desire for the HE line.

13

Accessories and Mango Touch

1. The function of accessories in fashion companies

According to the Oxford Dictionary, an accessory (as associated with fashion) is an adjunct to women's or men's clothing. Despite the definition, accessories have become the nucleus of the fashion economy, defining and distinguishing the appearance and nature of the individual.

Traditionally, accessories played a secondary role on the fashion catwalks, but in recent years they have produced very good financial results. In the case of Mango, accessory sales make up 10 per cent of total turnover.

At the end of the 20th century, accessories moved from being an exclusive addition in the world of mass production. They frequently abandoned their traditional purpose and instead represented a certain style or social class.

There is nothing new in this: at the end of the 18th century, fans, masks, wigs and alluring beauty marks played an important part in defining personal style. Thanks to these items, women were able to make an impression on men and their addition to a woman's wardrobe was essential for the game of love. Later, Coco Chanel established an important precedent in the design of accessories when she added jewellery to fashion. She was responsible for ensuring that accessories ceased to be the possessions of only the wealthy classes.Her long necklaces of pearls and rubies and her bracelets,all made with imitation stones, appealed to everybody. By creating costume jewellery and leaving aside the classical jewels of the past, value unconnected with the establishment of social class was added to individuality and personality, as the German philosopher Georg Simmel affirmed.

Beyond a doubt, accessories rose to the peak of democratization during the 1960s, when hats, handbags, court shoes and gloves became part of elaborate, formal and refined style, and shops began to offer affordable accessories to the general public. This was the rise of anti-luxury and ethnic *and* functional products.

Chanel, as we have noted, was the pioneer who discovered the power of the accessory as a decisive style factor. She created what was known as the 'total look' that went beyond just the clothes and that was not to be imitated by the rest of the fashion houses until the rise of marketing, at the beginning of the 1980s. It was during that decade that the fashion houses who were aiming for a more mass-sale and ready-to-wear approach discovered that their accessories could ensure that their brands, traditionally unaffordable, would reach the general public.

Great *haute couture* houses like Versace or Jean Paul Gaultier have been courageous enough to launch perfumes, makeup lines or sunglasses, renewing their offerings every one or two years. As pointed out by Santa Bartolomé Bertomeu, a professional specializing in fashion for over 30 years and professor at the European Design Institute, this factor intensified during the 1990s, when the big fashion companies' accessories lost a good part of their traditional function: helping to define the social position of the people who wore them. From then on, notwithstanding the threat to the great fashion houses' images or merchandising, the middle classes became a part of their target public. The need felt by the public to reinforce their identity by sporting accessories from big fashion companies has created an alternative market of copies and fakes that generates around 600 million Euros in Spain per year.

2. Mango and accessories

Mango has been a pioneer in taking advantage of the democratization of luxury in recent decades and the inexhaustible passion for accessories, since it has been successful in setting up points of sale or special spaces in existing shops which specialize in accessories.

Accessories have always played an important part in the Mango strategy. Their first store specializing in accessories opened in Valencia in 1997. This was the pilot Mango Accessories shop, and in the end, the company decided to include this line in its conventional points of sale.

In 2006, Mango Touch opened with a pilot store in a Madrid shopping centre. In 2007, shops of 40 square metres in size opened in Cannes and Toulouse, in the vicinity of the Mango stores. In the same year, new premises were opened in Spain, France, Russia and Andorra in keeping with an expansion plan which includes new shops in the future. So far, Touch is to be found in Andorra, Bahrain, Chile, Egypt, the United Arab Emirates, Spain, France, Lithuania, Qatar, Romania and Russia.

The Mango Touch shops reflect very feminine designs displayed in spaces which are warm and reassuring, lined in natural oak panelling. The furniture is dominated by a combination of styles, such as Louis XIV chairs, dark antique oak or or more modern wall cases with cleaner lines intended for the products.

Mango's aim is to create a chain of specific shops, distinguished from the competition by offering only its own products. The competitors have also identified the potential of this market, and a good example would be Inditex, which in 2007 launched a chain of stores specializing in fashion accessories under the brand name Uterqüe. In the same year, Benetton opened its first store dedicated solely to the sale of accessories, in Rome.

The design team entrusted with the accessories line consists of a large group of young people from a range of backgrounds and cultures that are divided into six work teams:

- Shoes

- Costume jewellery

- Sweet (a lingerie line intended also for street wear)

- Swimsuits

- Handkerchiefs

- Bags

The accessories line features two collections per year, autumn/winter and spring/summer. Even so, sometimes special one-off items appear as novelties, while those accessories that sell best are maintained throughout the year. As with clothing, two styles can also be seen for the accessories, one informal and the other more serious.

The accessories for sale in the Mango shops themselves are mainly located in two areas, depending on the size of the shop. For example, in the shop at Paseo de Gracia, 8 (Barcelona), we find some accessories near the tills (those appealing to more impulse-type buying, such as sunglasses, scarves and costume jewellery), while others, such as bags, shoes, lingerie and swimsuits, are in a separate area in the store interior.

Mango Touch products are manufactured in Spain, Turkey, India, China and Portugal.

As with the clothing lines, specific marketing strategies are adopted for the accessories. These strategies focus on the creation and positioning of the brand in collaboration with benchmark businesses and celebrities. Some examples would be the agreement signed with Nike for footwear or with Scarlett Johansson for the design of special bags intended to raise funds for the victims of the January 2010 Haiti earthquake. On other occasions, agreements have been signed with young designers with acknowledged international reputations.

Bibliography

- Case Studies:

  - ESADE Case Study: *Mango: The US market* (2004).

- Websites and magazine interviews:

  - Interview with Elena Carraso, Mango eBusiness director.

  - *Estudio sobre Usos de Internet en España 2009* [Study of the Uses of the Internet in Spain 2009] (Ministry for Industry, Commerce and Technology).

  - Interview with Damián Sánchez, *Esquire* (April 2010).

  - *Neo2,* Accessories special. Number 72.

- Periodical publications:

  - *Esade Alumni,* quarterly publication of the Association of Former ESADE Students, Autumn 2007, No. 122.

- Books:

  - Badía, Enrique. *Zara y sus hermanas* [Zara and her Sisters], LID Editorial Empresarial, 2009.

  - Blackman, Cally; *100 años de moda masculino* [100 Years of Men's Fashions]. Editorial Blume, 2009.

- Díaz Soloaga, Paloma. *El valor de la comunicación. Cómo gestionar marcas de moda* [The Value of Communication. How to Manage Fashion Brands]. First edition: July 2007. Cie Inversiones Editoriales Dossat 2000.

- Martínez Caballero, Elsa and Vázquez Casco, Ana Isabel. *Marketing de la moda* [Fashion Marketing]. Ediciones Pirámide, ESIC Editorial 2008.

- Roberts, Kevin. *LOVEMARKS, el futuro más allá de las marcas* [LOVEMARKS, the Distant Future of Brands]. Editorial Empresa Activa. 2005 Ediciones Urano, S.A.

- Teunissen, Jose and Brand, Jan; *Moda y accesorios* [Fashion and Accessories], Editorial Gustavo Gili, 2009.

- Thompson, EH, Pleck, JH and Ferrera, DL. *Men and masculinities: Scales for masculinity ideology and masculinity-related constructs.* Springer, 1992.

- Werle, Simone. *FASHIONISTA. A Century of Style Icons.* Editorial PRESTEL, 2009.

- Other sources:
  - Newspapers: *El Periódico, El Mundo, El País, Catalunya empresarial, etc.*
  - *Mango 2008* and *2009 annual reports.*
  - Interview by the authors with Enric Casi, CEO of Mango.
  - Mango Press Office.

ALSO PUBLISHED BY LID PUBLISHING:

WHEN GOD WASN'T WATCHING, THE DEVIL CREATED BUSINESS

ISBN: 9781907784001

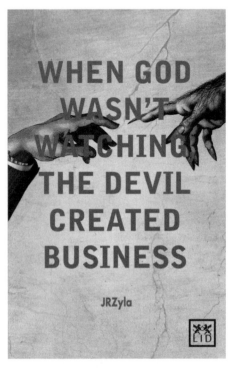

"This will be the cult book for modern executives and managers. Critical, tough and totally inspirational. An absolute eye-opener! You won't be able to put it down because you will feel the significance of the words so strongly."

David Peters, Managing Partner, CEO and Board Practice EMEA, Heidrick & Struggles International.

"This book strips business naked to expose what is good and what is terrible for the human being therein."

Max Landsberg, global bestselling author of *The Tao of Coaching and The Tools of Leadership.*

Does the modern corporate world, especially in times of crisis, resemble what we associate with heaven? Is working in business a heavenly experience or has it increasingly become the opposite? Business people everywhere, not only in executive management, are often working at their physical and emotional limits. It seems the Devil really did have a hand in creating modern business.

This book provides an honest and critical evaluation of our current business philosophies and management values, and looks at what has gone wrong. JRZyla further provides seven practical solutions to help you restore meaning and a higher degree of personal happiness in management and business today.

BEYOND
THE WRITTEN WORD

Authors who speak to you face to face.

Discover LID Speakers, a service that enables businesses to have direct and interactive contact with the best ideas brought to their own sector by the most outstanding creators of business thinking.

- A network specialising in business speakers, making it easy to find the most suitable candidates.

- A website with full details and videos, so you know exactly who you're hiring.

- A forum packed with ideas and suggestions about the most interesting and cutting-edge issues.

- A place where you can make direct contact with the best in international speakers.

- The only speakers' bureau backed up by the expertise of an established business book publisher.

402863